Praise for
Maybe a Note Would Help

"A testament to hope, illustrating the kind of transformative magic that can only occur by choosing to boldly step forward in the adventure of following our own unique idea."

—Amy Weinland Daughters, author of *Dear Dana* and *You Cannot Mess This Up*

"Written with heartfelt intention and deep compassion, *Maybe a Note Would Help* is a potent reminder of the enduring power of the written word."

—Priya Hutner, author of *Chasing Nirvana*

"There's finally a book that shows that sharing a note of encouragement is a delightful way to live. Kristen gives us practical examples that prove anyone can live a more intentional and meaningful life by incorporating note writing as part of your days."

—Jennifer Boyd, author of *Simple Hospitality*

". . . a helpful guide that highlights the power of thoughtful words in our lives and those with whom we share them."

—*Readers' Favorite*, 5-star review

Maybe a Note Would Help

Maybe a Note Would Help

Transforming Your Life with a Few Kind Words

KRISTEN TREMONTI REITER

SHE WRITES PRESS

Published in 2026 by
She Writes Press, an imprint of The Stable Book Group

32 Court Street, Suite 2109
Brooklyn, NY 11201
https://shewritespress.com
Library of Congress Control Number: 2026900515
ISBN: 979-8-89636-054-4
eISBN: 979-8-89636-055-1

Interior Designer: Tabitha Lahr

Printed in the United States

Names and identifying characteristics have been changed to protect the privacy of certain individuals.

To my Grandma Margaret,
whose unconditional love inspired me to love others.

To anyone who feels "a calling." However strange or lofty,
trust your intuition, and follow it wherever it leads you.

Contents

A Note from the Author

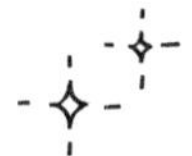

Dearest reader,

A quick note before you dig in: This book is a heartfelt exploration of writing, connection, discovery, and love. It was inspired and made possible by countless people, books, and moments that walked alongside me, not literally, but with my spirit and heart.

It was important that I included these inspirations because they were an integral part of my journey. They shaped me, inspired notes, provided strength and insights, and led me in the direction of love and expansion.

I hope the work and words of those who've inspired me might spark something inside of you. And who knows, maybe something in these pages will walk beside you too.

Thank you for taking a chance on Maybe a Note Would Help. Wishing you happy reading!

With my deepest gratitude,

Kristen

Prologue

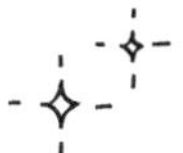

"Everybody is an answer to a prayer—we are all gifts and miracles to each other, even when we may not immediately see how that is so."

—David Cameron Gikandi, A Happy Pocket Full of Money

Eight months into my journey of writing a handwritten note every day for 365 days, I unknowingly crafted a note that would change the trajectory of my life. My partner, Austin, and I were on the lookout for a place to call our own, after a year of constantly moving around. Finally, we had decided to start the search for our dream home. The process wasn't easy, and we had made two unsuccessful backup offers before stumbling upon a hidden gem in Austin, Texas. This house was everything we had ever wished for: Nestled amid a mini forest, it was shaded by a beautiful live oak and cedar elm and felt like a modern-day tree house. It had an open concept with high ceilings and was located in an eclectic neighborhood with winding streets. As if that weren't enough, it was situated right across the street from a dog park!

I couldn't have imagined a more perfect place for us. To make sure the seller knew how much this house meant to us, I decided to write a handwritten note to accompany our offer:

To the owner,

We have long been on the search for a place to call home. When we toured yours, we knew we had found the one. The big trees, outdoor patios, and proximity to the dog park and trails won us over. We love to be outdoors with our nine-year-old pup, Sosa. Coming from Kansas and Florida, our hearts have been set on Austin. A place full of firsts, opportunity, and the perfect amount of weird. We would be honored to grow and create memories together on East Riverside.

Thank you for considering our offer, and wishing you the best on your next journey.

With gratitude,

Kristen, Austin, and Sosa

After an offer came in above ours, they gave us the chance to counter, which we did. We later received a text from the owner:

The letter and pics of you all and your pup clinched it for us! Y'all hit my soft spot.

We moved in two months later.

Who would have believed that one note could change everything? Of course, it wasn't that one note alone that did it. If I hadn't written a note every day that whole year, I might never have written that one.

Still, it blows my mind how something so simple can make such a big impact on my own life and the lives of others. A note is so small, yet the impact can be *huge*!

You can only imagine the actual number of lives you can touch by passing along joy, kindness, and love in the form of words like this. Today, we are (mostly) free to choose how we want to spend our time. Why not spend thirty minutes of your week writing handwritten notes? Try it, see if you like it.

Maybe writing notes will help you as it has helped me—to make stronger connections, to positively accelerate growth, and, ultimately, to achieve your dreams.

Introduction

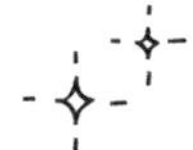

"There are two ways to live your life. One is as though nothing is a miracle. The other is as though everything is a miracle."

—Albert Einstein

While Austin and I were in Orlando for his NFL offseason training, I wrote a note to thank his sports agent, Bek, for taking care of us, our housing, and more for two months. Bek treated us not like a task he had to complete but like family he was thrilled to take care of. To recognize the "everyday miracles" he performed for us, it was the very least I could do to write a note to express our gratitude. I tried my best to write from the heart and to put my true feelings and thanks into words. My note, and his response, are below.

Bek,

Thank you for making our stay in Orlando so special and enjoyable. Our day at Discovery Cove was one of the best days of my life! Thank you for treating us to a fabulous dinner and a thrilling ride on the Wheel. I loved learning more about your life story and your family. It is incredible how you positively affect the life of everyone around you. Words will never be enough to express our gratitude for you. You are such a gift.

We love you,
Kristen and Austin

Hey guys!

I just received your postcard in the mail! I am speechless . . . not to say more.

My sister! Thank you so much. This is the best-written postcard I've ever received. Your card is full of love and full of gentleness. Thank you for such nice words. I love you both! I consider you family, and it will always remain this way. I love your heartfelt written card so much that I want to post it on IG. It's very special. . . . There is nothing I would want in return.

Thank you,
Bek

Receiving such positive, heartfelt feedback got me thinking. *I love writing notes. I love expressing my feelings through the written word. I love making people feel seen, acknowledged, and appreciated. It feels good writing notes. It feels good sending notes. So why don't I write handwritten notes even more often? What a simple and easy way to connect and to feel more connected in the world. If I could spread joy and love like this, then why the heck not? Bek is just one person who positively affects and impacts my life. Why don't I take the time to personally thank all the other people as well?*

After Bek sent his message, I had this realization: Writing notes is something I feel particularly skilled in *and* it brings me an unexplainable amount of joy. A win-win.

In fact, I wondered, *why don't I write 365 notes, one every day for one year, and see where it takes me?* I told Austin, and he said it would be cool *if I actually did it*. Challenge enthusiastically accepted. I was going to write a handwritten note every day for a year and see where it took me. I was eager and jazzed. And curious. What would this challenge look like? Where would it lead? I wasn't sure.

I don't get strong callings often. So, when I do, I know I must pay attention. I don't know where the inspiration came from—if it was desire, Source, or intuition—but I chose to listen. I knew this was the direction I needed to follow. I felt so strongly about this, I knew I had to start immediately. The time was now.

Life was up in the air for us at that moment, with Austin as a free agent and us living at his parents' house, with no end destination in sight. Over the next year, the ground under our feet constantly changed—we would live in Sarasota, New Orleans, Miami, Austin, and Kansas City. I didn't realize it then, but writing the notes would be the grounding mechanism I needed to get myself and us through that year. It was the best gift I could have ever given myself—a foundation for my mental, spiritual, and physical health during a period of constant transition as I lived out of a suitcase with no home base for six months.

Amid the chaos, I needed an avenue to spread joy and positivity. A practice to express the gratefulness I often felt but usually kept inside. Now I would put my thoughts into words and those words onto paper. I would send them to the people who had made an impact on my life in big ways, small ways, and everything in between. It would be my pleasure and honor to express thanks, support, love, or whatever I felt called to share with someone that day. This project gave me a way to dig a little bit deeper into my life experience.

The changes I went through in the process were bigger, and extended further, than I ever could have imagined. Unexpectedly, writing notes helped me overcome many mental health struggles. I wasn't in great shape, honestly. I had been medicated for anxiety and depression. In my twenties, I had engaged in countless toxic relationships with alcohol, people, and myself. At one time, it was commonplace for me to black out from drinking and cry, usually because I was terrified of ending up alone. I would try anything that promised to ease the deep pain I felt inside.

By this time, I had done years of therapy and self-work, but it was during this year of note-writing that my perspective really shifted. The practice helped me realize that I needed to make peace with myself and love myself. I needed to stop using substances and people to hide from myself and my problems. To escape. It became clear I needed to stop relying on the love of others to keep me afloat and instead take the time to put into words how grateful I was for the people I'd met along the way who kept me feeling and seeking the good in the world. It's a practice I've committed to. Without gratitude, I know what my life looks like. It's dark, lonely, and full of shame. Thankfully, I've found a more fulfilling way to live.

Through note-writing, and in turn, self-love, I have found a way to give back. To lean in more deeply. To savor the moments. To show my appreciation to everyone who has played a part in my becoming the best version of myself. My hope is that those people can feel my love and appreciation for them and their unique impact on my life. My goal is to create a ripple effect. To spread the joy and hope it keeps spreading.

I've always wanted to make a difference in the world, and I've never been exactly sure how to do it. As it turns out, sometimes all you need to do to change the world is to change yourself. Writing letters of love to all those who have left a footprint on my heart was my small start, allowing me to honor connection with those I've met, whose paths I truly believe I have crossed for a reason.

The notes were for me in many ways, but they were also about others—about seeing them, acknowledging them, honoring their value, and finding a common thread and humanness between us. They helped me recognize the love that is constantly surrounding me. The notes brought me joy, connection, and confidence, and filled my cup. They helped me see the goodness in others and the goodness in myself. They made me feel less alone.

With all that I've gained from my experiment in note-writing, I'm confident that you, too, can find a way to interact more vividly with your life, engage more fully, and make sense of your journey through handwritten notes. I'm willing to bet that your note-writing will help you uplift others to a higher degree of self-appreciation and in turn make you feel better in your own skin.

So, how do you do it? If you're anything like me, you'll need a plan.

I'm not much of a rule follower (ha!), but I did give myself some guidelines for this project to help me stay connected to the outside and also to my inside. I found this simple strategy to be a biohack for connection:

- Write 365 notes, one every day for one year
- Write them to whoever I want or feel called to write to that day
- Once a month, write to different aspects or versions of myself
- Deliver the notes in person or send them via snail mail, if possible

Once the plan was in place, it wasn't hard to get started. I had plenty of people I wanted to thank from my past—teachers, coaches, and coworkers who had made an impact on my life. I could also write to people in my present life—my partner, grocery workers, neighbors, and all the people I had daily encounters with in big ways and small.

Consistently keeping up the practice was a little more challenging. But my intention was to create meaningful connections and to deepen my relationships with others, my environment, all living beings, and in turn, myself, and I understood that this required committing to an everyday practice—setting aside time each day to use my words, to express what was on the inside. Sometimes that was gratitude, joy, and appreciation. Sometimes it was support, comfort, and understanding. Sometimes it was silliness, play, and poetry.

Every day I showed up differently, as will you. The world changes, and we change. Everything, including us, is in constant flux. Fighting change is too hard; believe me, I've tried. It's much simpler to go with the flow, to focus on what I can control. And that's showing up every day with a pen and paper.

I focused my energy on finding the good. There were days I would smile, write a note to my dog that brightened my heart, and read it to him out loud. There were days I would cry when my partner was in pain, and I'd write to him to express my love and support. There were days when people lost loved ones, and I wrote to send them love and offer them comfort.

Little did I know when I started that the year ahead would continue to be full of uncertainty, challenges, and constant change. Our housing situation was up in the air for many months, for example. But there was one thing I could count on, and that was sitting down, wherever we were, and crafting my note—having a daily practice of connecting more deeply. To someone else. To my environment. To life. To myself. To my place in the world. I didn't know it at the time, but this was exactly what I needed to keep me going.

My note-writing was the calling I didn't know I needed. As a person who previously used medication to cope—to live, sleep, and pretty much do anything—I needed this avenue to stay present. It provided something positive and life-giving to keep me from sinking into my previous vices. I am so grateful that my higher self, Source, God, and my intuition led me here.

Life is wild, unpredictable, and uncertain for all of us. And I knew where living unconsciously and depending on substances and vices got me. Maybe you know it too; it's not a good place.

But this journey takes us to a good place. A better place. The best place? Maybe so. Certainly, my values and intuition have realigned, my relationships have evolved, and my mental health has improved. My creativity has blossomed, I've gotten better at expressing myself, and I've helped others do the same. I've become grounded and embodied love; I've felt purposeful and expansive. So it's no wonder that after my 365 days (and more) of handwritten notes, I'm hooked.

I realize my language around note-writing can sound romantic, my enthusiasm a bit over-the-top. I confess I do find note-writing romantic. But it is also a practical tool, grounded in the everyday. Writing handwritten notes is an actionable method for making the world just a little bit brighter and better. We can all benefit from notes of encouragement and support, and we can all write them. That's why I'm passionate about spreading the good note-writing news; I hope to revive the lost art and to flood the mail with handwritten notes.

On the way to that goal, I'd like to invite you to join me in the handwritten-note revolution. In this book, I'll show you exactly how to do it. I'll share what I've discovered on my journey and, hopefully, inspire you through my experience. I'll also offer a practical, step-by-step guide showing you exactly what to do. In these pages, I hope to accompany you as you begin to feel more deeply connected to yourself, your life, others, and the world around you.

Before we dive deeper, I want to clarify for anyone wondering what I mean, exactly, by a "note." In my definition, a note is any creative and meaningful written message given to express thoughtfulness and appreciation and to convey sincere wishes. In parts of this book, I refer to a note using the words “card” or “letter.” These words are interchangeable.

It’s that easy. This isn’t rocket science. Writing a note is a simple way to exponentially increase connection and use our words to empower others, to intentionally reach out, vulnerabilities and all, and to create deeper connections with the world and with ourselves.

You may be surprised by what you learn along the way. Sometimes I didn’t even know how I felt about someone until I put the words on paper, until I set aside time to do nothing else but think about that person, how they made me feel and the unique gifts they had to offer—the gifts that made them *them*. My words sometimes surprised me too. I didn’t consciously realize how deeply some people had influenced my life until the words came out. In order for this to happen, though, I had to create a container for it. This forced me to get creative, to dig more deeply into myself, and to pull out the feelings that were in there.

My goal is to inspire more handwritten notes. And through them, to create meaningful, intentional connections. To do this, we’ll need to build an army of note-writing warriors, spreading love and light with their paper and pens. To inspire expression and creativity. To spread joy and love. To uncover truth and wonder.

These notes we’ll write are the opposite of the shallow, impersonal falseness we find online. People are hungry for genuine connection. This is important work, for we need each other more than ever. Please join me.

Part I:

Learning Curve

With any new skill or practice comes a learning curve. You crawl before you walk. You walk before you run. You know the deal here. I will take you along on my journey of discovery, my learning curve, in Part I. It's the "why." It's the rhyme and reason. It's the juicy background info and benefits. Don't worry, we will get to the "how" in Part II. So buckle up, sit back, and enjoy the note-writing ride.

Chapter One:

Getting Grounded

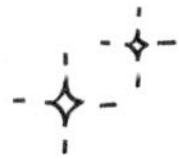

"Focus on building the most meaningful life you can, in whatever situation you're in."

—Oliver Burkeman, *Four Thousand Weeks: Time Management for Mortals*

My "official" 365-day journey with handwritten notes began with a simple gesture of gratitude. I wrote my first note to our friends in Austin, Texas, thanking them for hosting us and telling them how much I cherished our time together. How they made it feel like home.

Meg and Mark,

Thank you for hosting a wonderful weekend full of adventure and fun. I am in constant awe of your hospitality and kindness. You are both upstanding humans, and I truly cherish the time we spend together. Thank you for sharing your home, lake house, delicious eats, dance moves, creativity, stories, laughs, and city with us. My heart is happy and full. Please give Reddy a boop on the nose from us. We love you!

Love,
Kristen and Austin

Before I started my note-writing journey, nothing felt like home because my partner, Austin, was an NFL free agent, so our living situation was at the mercy of a football team—and we weren't sure which one. We were not homeless, although we did not have a place to live or call our own.

Football free agency typically starts in the middle of March each year. When a player is not under contract with a team, they are free to sign with any NFL team that makes them an offer they are willing to accept. Austin was a free agent for the first time since we had met. We moved away from Kansas City after he turned down a deal to play with the Chiefs, and after starting on two Super Bowl teams, he was ready to test the waters of free agency. This meant waiting for an unknown period of time until another team made an offer. We waited for the call, hoping for the best. It was a difficult and unsettling time.

While Austin trained, we were living at his parents' house in Sarasota, Florida, which was under construction. We were far away from Kansas City—our home for the past three years—far from my friends, my family, my job, and our football community. We found ourselves alone together, walking on green concrete floors while listening to the all-day symphony of jackhammering, strange footsteps, and paintbrushes. All the while, the walls literally came down around us. Our lifestyle slowed down significantly, coming to an abrupt halt in the land of retirees. We had expected Austin to sign with a team during the first week or two of this period in March, but it didn't happen. Our life was not going as we had planned. Uncertainty filled our days, and I found myself crying on most of them.

We yearned for a home base—somewhere we could weather the storm of free agency. I was tired of people feeling sorry for us and constantly asking if we had any news. We didn't. They would ask us what was next. We didn't know. We were in a strange limbo, waiting for good news that never seemed to come. This continued from March through April, May, June, July, August, and into the beginning of the football season.

I was tired of football running our lives—dictating where we lived, where we could go, and when. We turned down trips with friends in case a team called, which meant Austin would have to fly there for a workout the same day. I was run-down and dispirited. I felt disconnected from myself and my community in Kansas City. I worked hard to stay afloat, using every skill in my toolbox. Even so, I was drowning in despair. Austin and I clung to each other during this difficult time, hoping and having faith that it wouldn't last forever.

These uncertain times were dim, and I longed to find my light again. I needed some joy to shine away the gray. On June 16, 2021, three months into our "homeless" limbo, I knew in my bones that it was time to reach out, to take the first step toward connecting with people again. That's when I wrote my first note, the one to Meg and Mark that opens this chapter.

And by doing that, I discovered that being away from your people helps you realize how much you truly appreciate them. So I continued to write notes to Austin's family, other friends, and my family. I stretched further and wrote to our Airbnb host, our white water rafting guide, and one of my favorite music artists. Where life would take me was uncertain—as it is for all of us humans—so I leaned into what I could control. Every day, I could do this one meaningful thing: reach out to let people know how much I valued their presence in my life. These notes became my anchor.

My note-writing practice carried me through many question marks and challenges. It grounded me in gratefulness and helped me ride the roller coaster of life. It was the seatbelt I needed to keep me safe and secure, even when the ride felt a little too exhilarating for comfort—bumpy and wild.

Three months after my first note, Austin signed with the New Orleans Saints. Ironically, just like us, the entire Saints organization was displaced due to the hurricane. They set up shop in Texas before eventually moving back to New Orleans. I visited Austin in Texas before I drove from Florida with our dog to temporarily live in the Loews Hotel in downtown New Orleans. Less than a month later, I was dropping Austin off at the airport and packing up our pup to make the drive back to Florida because he was signed by the Miami Dolphins.

Once again, we would need to find a new place to live. Adding to the challenge, the place needed to be one that would take us *and* our furry companion, our sweet dog, Sosa. He's gentle and loving, but because he is considered a "pit bull–type dog," Sosa is subject to breed restrictions in many places. This made finding housing especially difficult, and we often had to sneak him into hotels, which kept me on high alert.

Everything was in a constant state of flux. I never knew what state we would be in next. It's no wonder I often felt discombobulated and overwhelmed.

Celebrating Slowness

Do you ever experience that discombobulated and overwhelmed feeling too? Like the world is moving too fast and you can hardly keep up? Like everything is changing so rapidly that you can hardly wrap your mind around the latest reality shift? This feeling snuck up on me often during this time. My equalizing skills were constantly being put to the test, and as I was frequently on edge and disconnected from a sense of stability, I often failed to adapt as gracefully as I would have liked. I was trying to move too fast.

Fortunately, writing handwritten notes provided a remedy. Note-writing is exactly the opposite of moving too fast; it's about celebrating slowness. Soaking in the meaning and effort and enjoying the process along the way. Writing handwritten notes is not the most efficient or fastest way to communicate. You will not be able to reach as many people as you would with a mass text or email. But that's the point. Going too fast has done nothing positive for our relationships, our communities, or our world. Why do we keep trying to replace intention, effort, and meaning with speed?

Slowing down is the answer. We should aim to be more like the tortoise in the old fable—investing in ourselves and others by taking the time to slow down, look around, and appreciate the journey and those on the journey with us. To pay closer attention with intention. We are all in this together, after all, and we are all headed to the same place eventually (spoiler alert: There's no prize for whoever makes it to the grave first). There is no need to rush. We might as well enjoy the ride and take care of each other along the way.

Maybe the notes worked because a handwritten note is like the tortoise, and a text message is like the hare. They are both moving forward, but in distinctly different ways. The tortoise is slow and purposeful. The tortoise does not rush; instead, it takes its time and enjoys every step of the way. Moving at its own steady pace with intention, the tortoise allows the journey to unfold naturally. This is mindfulness in action.

With the opposite approach, the hare is fast and wants to get to the finish line as quickly as possible. The hare speeds through life, not looking around to enjoy the ride. Speed is the only goal; the journey itself is mostly forgotten. We all know how this story ends.

I am as guilty as anyone of falling into the efficiency trap. I refuse to make two trips from the car after going to the grocery store. I used to mass text everyone in my phone book on holidays because I wanted to make sure they knew I was thinking about them and that they mattered. There is nothing inherently wrong with this. My heart was in the right place, and it was the best way I knew to reach out at the time.

Through the note-writing experience, I've found that sometimes less is more. Instead of an impersonal text blast to everyone whose phone number I've ever gathered, I can write a small number of handwritten personal notes to a select few people. It will surely take more time, and the reach won't be as wide (unless I'm really trying to give my writing hand a workout), but I think it holds more meaning.

Building a Lifeline

I had a choice to make. I could either face this challenging, uncertain, ungrounding time with fear and retreat into the safety of my shell, or I could transform adversity into something beautiful. I could create something special that I could be proud of. Harnessing that nervous energy and redirecting it into a practice that would help ground me through the days, I began to build a lifeline to the world. A lifeline back to myself. I realized that instead of sinking, I could float with my handwritten-note life preserver.

And so I dove headfirst into the year of writing.

I felt a magnetic pull toward a brighter path—a path that would improve my well-being, nurture positivity, and enrich my existence. Each note became a precious gift, a keepsake that could be cherished by its recipient, whether displayed on a refrigerator or tucked away in a drawer, offering comfort during tough times. These notes also became a gift to myself, a tangible reminder of the abundance of goodness in my life, amplifying my gratitude and awareness. I was called to recognize the everyday gifts surrounding me, if only I could truly see and acknowledge them. Writing notes gave me a way to express my thoughts, create something from nothing, and find joy again from the inside out.

Reviving a Lost Art

In a digital world where we can easily get lost, the practice of hand-writing notes assumes a sacred role as a resource and tool to help us stay present and aware in our lives. It provides an avenue for us to regain consciousness and experience our emotions more deeply. To feel deeper into the feels. It allows us to lean into our reality, to open our hearts not only to others but to ourselves. Through the art of capturing our thoughts and sentiments, we reclaim our existence in the world with greater appreciation.

As I have freely admitted, I do tend to romanticize handwritten notes. How can you not? There is something about the personalization that I think is just dreamy. It's your unique gifts and words in their own creative form. The notes are a reflection of your personality, character, and writing style that captures a glimpse of your unique relationship with the recipient. A heartfelt expression of authenticity. An act of beauty. An intimate, physical experience with a pen and paper.

Your personally handwritten note is inimitable. No one will ever write the same note, with your words, with your handwriting, with your sentiment, with your energy. Your time, effort, and attention to detail are intentionally and deliberately focused on the receiver, making it a unique and sentimental gift nobody else can give, because you are giving of yourself.

That's why handwritten notes simply cannot be replaced by texts, emails, or e-cards. The personal touch cannot be reproduced in digital communications. Hand-writing notes conveys a thoroughly human sense of thoughtfulness and care. There is nothing like it in the world. It cannot be replaced by AI.

Note-writing is truly an art—a lost art that deserves to be found. The world needs your art, your one-of-a-kind masterpieces, your handwritten notes.

So I invite you to make a regular practice of writing notes. You might write one note every day for one year as I did, or your schedule might be different. You can start with baby steps, knowing that even something so small, so simple, as writing one single note has the capacity to bring big things. The gifts will pour out like clowns from a clown car: joy, appreciation, connection, value, and love. I promise you: Positivity will flow no matter how you begin—you just have to start.

And take it slow. When you are tempted to convey your message quickly, think again about the benefits of writing mindfully. The more thoughtful you are, the more deeply the receiver will appreciate it; a note from the heart feels better, and it means more.

Chapter Two:

Cultivating Connection

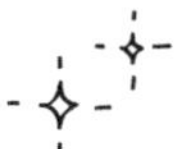

"Our daily moments of connection with others are the tiny engines that drive the upward spiral between positivity and health."

—Barbara Fredrickson, "Social Connections Drive the 'Upward Spiral' of Positive Emotions and Health"

At first, I thought my calling was solely about the notes. Looking closer, I realized it was actually a call to connect on a deeper level—with myself, with others, with my environment, and with the world around me. My calling to connect was my intuition nudging me to come back to my roots, to myself. To find my joy again from the inside and to sprinkle it around the world like confetti.

The notes, like this one to my friends' daughter, were just serving as the vessel to transport me there.

Blake,

Hello, my long-lost friend! Kristen and Sosa here, writing to you from the sunny state of Florida. How is your summer going so far? What has been making you happy lately? We have been riding Go-Peds around the neighborhood, and

I've been eating animal crackers. Speaking of animals, I've been seeing a lot of new species down here. There are three wood storks (they are endangered!) that I like to visit in the mornings. They hang out high up in the tree down our street. I've gone to see them in the afternoon, but they are never there. Only in the mornings! There are also sandhill cranes in the lake behind our house. They make funny noises. Your mom showed me the bookmark you made her. It is super neat. You are an artist! What else have you been creating? I hope you are having an awesome summer full of fun and laughs. If you want to write me back, my address is below.

Friends forever,

Kristen

PS—This pen is scented and smells like strawberry!

Missed Connections

Why does it seem so hard to make these kinds of connections today? As a social species, our innate human need for connection has not changed over time. As always, we want to be seen, known, and loved. We want to be acknowledged. We want to feel good about ourselves. We want to feel connected and a part of something bigger. We want to know we are worthy.

A handwritten note can meet those needs, but too few of us send or receive them. According to the *Daily Mail*, the average US household receives a personal letter just once every seven weeks. Compare that to 1987 when the average household received a letter every two weeks.[1]

1. "You Haven't Got Mail: Average US households receive a personal letter just once every seven weeks," Daily Mail Online, October 3, 2011, https://www.dailymail.co.uk/news/article-2044652/Average-US-households-receive-personal-letter-just-7-weeks.html.

We do receive mail, but what kind? Advertising. According to CompareCamp.com, advertising mail accounted for 62 percent of all mail received by households in the United States in 2018.[2] When you walk to your mailbox and open it up, what do you see? Mostly bills and coupons, "Let us buy your house" mail, "Vote for so and so" political ads, etc. When I receive a handwritten note, I am jazzed up. What a break from the rest of the junk. It's a reminder that I exist and matter to people besides the bill collectors.

Once upon a time, handwritten notes and letters were among the few ways of delivering news quickly over long distances. The humans and horses of the famous Pony Express risked their lives for these handwritten messages, sending horse-mounted riders from Missouri to California. It was an innovative and risky venture that acknowledged the importance of these cross-country messages.

Many things have changed in the last 150 years. Everything is faster and more efficient, but are we better for it? What we've done is make it easier to communicate without much thought. Meanwhile, note-writing has almost fallen off our cultural radar entirely.

Still, we don't have to go back to the 1860s to find a time when communications were more intimate, more meaningful—just back to my high school days! As my high school best friends can confirm, I took socializing more seriously than school. And before smartphones and unlimited texting became available, I had two choices: talk to a person in between classes, or write them a note. My friends and I wrote hundreds, maybe thousands, of notes throughout our four years there. It was a cute and pure way to connect, although not without risk: We developed a stealth system of passing notes hand to hand or tossing the

---

2. Andrew Zuckerman, "40 Direct Mail Statistics: 2020/2021 Behavior, Trends & Data Analysis," *CompareCamp.com*, May 21, 2020, https://comparecamp.com/direct-mail-statistics/.

note between our desks and hoping for a smooth landing so the teachers couldn't catch us and, more importantly, so that none of the juicy details we shared would make it into the wrong hands.

I still have some of these notes, decorated with doodles and drawings and special lettering and filled with cartoons and calligraphy, updates on life, big shares, and lots of questions. My friends and I shared inside jokes and played games. My high school boyfriend would write me poems, which he would spray with his cologne. We found cool ways to fold the paper like origami. We spent time making the notes special and fun for each other. We also shared our thoughts, feelings, secrets, hopes, and dreams. Even our apologies.

We loved connecting through notes, and our relationships thrived. The notes helped us deepen our bonds, express ourselves, and make more sense of the world as we were treading through it. They were our lifelines to each other. Receiving a note in between classes was the best. I loved knowing that someone was thinking of me enough to write me an entire note full of their loving energy, their voice, their character, their writing style, their sense of humor—their whole essence. And they wanted to share it with me. I can't imagine a better gift.

I proudly carried my notes with me to the next class and devoured every word, secretly reading them when I should have been paying attention in class. I cherished my relationships above everything, especially school. Of course, I would secretly write back, pretending to take "school notes." The teachers didn't catch on that my notes were not school related. I am proud of high school me—even then, I was holding my value of note-writing high. Think about it. Would you rather receive a "love text" or a "love letter"? Is one more meaningful than the other? I think so.

We should revive the age-old practice of writing handwritten notes to help us connect with others and the world around us in a more meaningful and authentic way. And for posterity—historically, handwritten letters have been kept and passed down through generations. These notes help us connect across time. That doesn't seem likely with texts.

But what of the additional thought and hassle and the greater difficulty of writing by hand? The "inconvenience" of note-writing? We're used to modern efficiency—whether through email, Slack, text, or any other modern technology. But consider what we've lost by moving toward convenience: meaning. We've taken away the very effort that makes writing and sending a handwritten note so meaningful.

With unlimited options for how to spend our time, it matters when we consciously choose to put the extra effort into crafting a thoughtful communication of lovingkindness for someone else. In the modern world, giving someone our attention, when it's constantly being pulled in a million different directions, can only strengthen that relationship. It's a connection builder. The purest form of generosity. The ultimate expression of love.

Social Media

So, you might agree with me that email and text are soulless ways to communicate compared to handwritten notes, but what about the digital landscape that was created for the very purpose of connecting people—social media? Shouldn't that work better? Maybe it should, but I don't think it does. In fact, I agree with Wednesday Addams in Netflix's *Wednesday* when she says, "I find social media to be a soul-sucking void of meaningless affirmation."

For example, at the beginning of my relationship with Austin, I had a small meltdown and confided in my best friend, Annie. I had noticed that the red heart symbol had disappeared next to Austin's name on Snapchat. What did this mean?! (For those unfamiliar with Snapchat, the red heart indicates that two individuals send more snaps and photos to each other than anyone else and are "best friends.")

I was beside myself. In my distressed state, I failed to realize the absurdity of using a digital symbol to gauge the strength of a relationship.

My mind raced with worries. Was my boyfriend snapping other girls? And if so, was he snapping them more than me? I started concocting a scenario in my head, envisioning a mysterious girl who might be seeing the red heart next to his name, instead of me. Were *they* best friends on Snapchat now? Was our relationship over? Was this the end? Was I out? And was *she*, whoever she was, in?

Annie, similar to Wednesday Addams, couldn't give two shits about social media and brought me back down to earth. I was freaking out about an application on a phone that lets us send photos that disappear in seconds. This was not an accurate measure of closeness. The red heart was not an indicator of how real our real-life relationship was. It wasn't a good reason for crying and drowning in self-pity and feelings of a lack of "enoughness."

What a silly thing to worry about, truly, but it was so real to me at the time. I don't think I'm alone in losing sleep over social media and suffering from the stress and strain it causes on real-life relationships. After all, we are all looking for connection. It's just that social media cultivates a false sense of connection, a cheap, fake, artificial-belonging feeling. Processed connection. You can't hack deep and meaningful relationships. At least, not in my experience. True connections and genuine relationships require time, effort, and vulnerability.

I yearned to relate to other humans in a real way. In deeply fulfilling and meaningful ways. Faster, manufactured connection was—and is—not the answer. Believe me, I've tried, and that ain't it. Slower, intentional connection is. Did someone say snail mail?

Do you also feel a lack of connection as you navigate the ever-expanding digital landscape? Do you feel isolated physically, mentally, or emotionally? Do you worry that your connections with the people in your life aren't deep enough? That your connections aren't genuine? Are you looking for more meaning? More purpose? More fulfillment? More joy? If so, you are not alone.

Writing handwritten notes can be a catalyst for the connection you are seeking. Taking on this practice will reacquaint you with what has been lost within yourself, within your environment, and with others: intentional, meaningful connection from one person to another. It is a simple service that fulfills the innate human need to see and to be seen. Writing a handwritten note is affirming for you and is appreciated by the receivers. As Carl W. Buehner said, "People may forget what you say. They may forget what you did, but people will never forget how you made them feel." This is the why.

Writing handwritten notes helped me feel less isolated by linking my little world back into my community and into others' worlds. Removing the separation, one note at a time, made me feel less alone and more fulfilled. It helped me create meaning.

You can do the same. Through admiration, appreciation, thoughtfulness, and gratitude, you have the opportunity to connect more deeply with the human spirit. This will make you feel more at peace within yourself and more at one with the world. You will find joy and feel love by giving it. Small gifts of words can spark new friendships and strengthen the ones you already have. Forming those words can help you see the world with new eyes and feel grateful for life and your part in it.

There is infinite room in the world for deeper meaning and connection, far beyond the social media landscape. Handwritten notes are calling us to participate. "Help people feel acknowledged and seen! You will feel more connected to the world . . . just pick up your pen and paper and start writing us!" the notes beg.

Healing Through Connection

As humans, feeling grounded is essential to our survival and our well-being. Studies show that connectedness has far-reaching physical implications, from relieving pain to enhancing the function of our nervous systems. Dr. Vivek Murthy, the author of *Together: The Healing Power of Human Connection in a Sometimes Lonely World*, discovered that a lack of connection with others is the most common condition people suffer from, regardless of their background or status. And reclaiming that connection is good medicine. According to Dr. Emma Seppala, feeling connected to others can lower levels of anxiety and depression while increasing self-esteem, empathy, and trust, leading to more openness and cooperation.[3] In other words, social connectedness generates a positive feedback loop of communal, emotional, and physical well-being. This connection helps us feel stable, centered, and anchored in our lives.

I'm living proof. When I started writing handwritten notes, I no longer felt like I was alone on an island. Writing notes gave me a safe way to connect, to see others, and to be seen in return, even in the simplest of everyday interactions. For example, I wrote notes to the groundskeeper, leasing agents, handy people, and neighbors at our apartment complex

3. Emma Seppala, Phd., "Connectedness & Health: The Science of Social Connection," *The Center for Compassion and Altruism Research and Education,* May 8, 2014.

in Miami. They felt seen and appreciated. Instead of being strangers, we became friends. I began to feel like I belonged exactly where I was; I was not stranded alone on an island but part of an active and heartfelt community.

Through my year of note-writing, I discovered human connection is nature's medicine. Perhaps I shouldn't have been so surprised. After all, the Harvard Study of Adult Development has found that personal connections are *the* most important factor in long-term health and happiness. "Contrary to what many people might think," write the study's authors, "it's not career achievement or exercise, or a healthy diet. Don't get us wrong; these things matter. But one thing continuously demonstrates its broad and enduring importance: good relationships."[4]

By investing in your relationships, you are investing in your own health and well-being. What's magical is that the healing effects don't stop with you—they will spread to note recipients, your circle, those you come into contact with, and more. With handwritten notes, we can learn to heal people without physically touching them. With handwritten notes, we can nourish, love, and heal ourselves and our world. It's like therapy, but much cheaper.

The Community Cure

Writing handwritten notes is a remedy for countless ailments, especially loneliness. Loneliness appears to be a Western epidemic—it has been proven to be a dangerous threat to our health and well-being. We all felt it during the COVID lockdowns and in the aftermath, whether physically, mentally,

4. Robert Waldinger and Marc Schulz, "The Real Secret of Lifelong Fulfillment," *The Wall Street Journal*, February 3, 2023, https://www.wsj.com/story/the-real-secret-of-lifelong-fulfillment-6c1d026a.

or emotionally. But even without the influence of COVID, loneliness is a huge problem in our modern world. According to the Roots of Loneliness Project, 52 percent of Americans report feeling lonely, while 47 percent report their relationships with others are not meaningful.[5] Americans are sick with loneliness, and we collectively need to make changes. And though quick Band-Aid fixes are abundant, I urge you to look elsewhere for help.

I speak from experience. I used quick fixes like alcohol to ease my anxiety and depression. After college, my alcohol consumption was heavy, and I kept it up through my twenties without realizing it was a problem. However, the longer I used alcohol to become unconscious to my own reality, the more disconnected from myself and my intuition I became. I constantly questioned myself and my decisions. And the temporary highs became lasting lows. There are black holes in my memory I will never be able to get back. I often felt ashamed and confused.

I began taking antidepressants. They dulled the pain enough that I could crawl out of the hole I'd fallen into, but I became dependent on them at night to sleep. I was functioning, although I was not feeling like the face of health and wellness. The COVID pandemic only compounded my troubles, as restaurants, offices, and gyms closed down, taking my daily routine along with them. Without access to my gym, my usual outlet, I was thrown for a loop. I was faced with myself again, the person I had been running away from all of these years.

As COVID ran rampant, so did my anxiety. The panic-inducing messages were everywhere: Wear a mask! Remain a physically safe distance from other people! It's not safe out there!

---

5. Christie Hartman, "Loneliness Statistics: By Country, Demographics & More," *The Roots of Loneliness Project*, June 9, 2023, https://www.rootsofloneliness.com/loneliness-statistics.

I struggled to adapt, to handle the uncertainty and anxiety. My mind was a hostile environment, and I held myself to impossible standards of perfection, further fueling my anxiety. I was never good enough for myself; I was an unreasonably tough critic. I had to be successful, kind, and purposeful. Somewhere in my mind, perfection was attainable if I just kept striving for it. And you bet I was going to try!

I coped with the pressure in some unhealthy ways. In addition to antidepressants, I took Adderall to get shit done. My to-do list grew small and so did I. I dropped three jean sizes. A dear friend asked me if everything was OK. I was offended. Of course I was OK. Wasn't it obvious I was doing great, looking perfect, and keeping everything together?

I did not have it all together. In fact, all the striving zapped my energy.

I was operating in a way that could not continue forever. Antidepressants in the morning to wake up, Adderall to keep me going all day, and another antidepressant at night to sleep. Repeat. I had to make a change. I wanted to move forward, away from the grayness of life, and see colors again. I had to be brave enough to deal with my own shit, to face my feelings and sit with them instead of dulling them out. I had to reconnect with myself and my intuition and hope it would show me the way—or at least the next step. One foot in front of the other, I had to find new and different ways to move forward.

I knew that antidepressants and Adderall were not long-term answers to my inner turmoil, so I safely discontinued them. (Please note, I am not a doctor, and I am not advising you to get off any medications. My intention is to shine a light on how common it is to prescribe a quick fix or pill without digging deeper into underlying issues.)

It was scary to step into the unknown again, but my motivation was strong. I wanted to be free to feel whatever was coming through, to face the inevitable bumps in the road, and to feel like myself again. I was excited to get back to who I was—highs, lows, and all. I was tired of the gray and ready for the colors. I was ready to *live* again. Fully.

So I ripped off the Band-Aid and started paying attention to the deeper issues—my disconnection from myself and from others. I added new medicines to my cabinet, including meditation and other spiritual practices. Most importantly, I started self-medicating with handwritten notes.

Through the notes, I began to feel more like myself, the person I was meant to be. Even though I was still in this limbo world where I couldn't wrap my head around what was next for me, for us, I could take a small step back to focus on a simple task that I could handle. Writing the notes helped me connect with others while I was not physically present with them, and it provided me with a creative, fulfilling purpose and healed my heart in a way that quick fixes never could.

Here's how I coached myself in the form of a handwritten note:

> *Feeling down? Write a note. Missing your family across the country? Write them a note. Can't see your grandma because of COVID? Write her a note. Feeling anxious? Write a note to your anxiety. Feeling strong and empowered? Write a note to your ex and thank them for everything they taught you. Feeling jazzed about the latest podcast you listened to? Write that person a note! Feeling seen after reading Brené Brown's new book? Write her a note!*

As I wrote, I slowly realized I could be my own source of strength and love, and that's when I began to see the colors in life again. I was able to let go of my self-imposed pressure and expectations and focus on what mattered. I learned that ripping off the Band-Aid and facing your issues can be scary, but it's ultimately the best way to heal.

Y'all, it was incredible to discover that there were so many people who affected my life meaningfully on the daily. My spirit ignited with connection, and that sparked both my creativity and my ability to put it into action to spread love. I felt the gratitude fill my heart and spill through the rest of my body. It felt good!

Do I still have bad days? Yes, every week before I start my period I feel like the sky is falling. Does note-writing help? Absolutely. I experience joyful moments throughout the entire process. The joy begins with thinking about it and continues through the act of writing the first draft of the note. The good feels roll into the actual writing of the note (FUN!) and the love and TLC that go into it. Sometimes I cry because I'm so excited and because of the heartfelt-ness. Sending out the note? Especially fun! And then the bonus joy when people reach back out to tell me they received it and how it touched them. That is joy so many times!

Handwritten notes are the new antidepressants. It makes sense. As we've seen, connection is a pillar of health. Maybe we should get doctors and therapists to prescribe note-writing! Or maybe I'll be the Note Doctor, prescribing note-writing for whatever ails you. On my prescription pad, I'd be sure to write something like this: "Beware of the side effects: joy, fulfillment, love, happiness, connection, and community. Warning: Please report back if you feel *too much joy*."

When we heal and grow, it's not only our lives we are changing but also the lives of our families, our friends, and our communities. It spreads to everyone around us and continues to spread like ripples in open water. Like wildfire.

Chapter Three:

Reinforcing Relationships

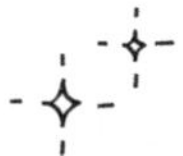

"Time modifies all human relationships for better or for worse, depending upon the policy through which people relate themselves to one another."

—Napoleon Hill, *Outwitting the Devil: The Secret to Freedom and Success*

It was my first Thanksgiving away from my family. As a sentimental person, I had FOMO. I wanted to be there in person, to celebrate with the people I cherished the most. To share food and memories. To catch up on life happenings, to laugh, to see who was overserved by the end of the night. Until then, I had taken our holiday togetherness for granted, never realizing how truly special it was to simply be together, share a meal, and celebrate together in person. I was feeling especially alone knowing my family's Thanksgiving would go on without me. So I wrote them a note.

Tremontis,

The first Thanksgiving away from my family. The people I cherish the most. Although family is given, mine is also chosen. Every step of the way. Thank you for being my people. My support system when I am down, my cheerleaders through the victories, and every day in between. I hit the jackpot. I am grateful to experience life with you, Mom, Dad, Andrew, and Elise. Thank you for being you. You are all imperfectly perfect to me and I love you with my whole heart.

Happy Thanksgiving,
Kristen and Sosy

After writing this note to them I felt full of gratitude, knowing I had special people, that our bond could not be separated by physical distance.

Relationships as Multipliers

The quality of our relationships determines the quality of our lives. That's because, as Mark Manson says, relationships are the multipliers of life, making good things even better and bad things even worse.[6] Considering their significant impact on our lives, it's important to take steps to improve them. If we don't proactively invest in them, they will slowly deteriorate. Writing handwritten notes is an effective and actionable way to nurture our relationships and strengthen them over time.

For me, writing notes has been a transformative experience in countless ways, and one of the most delightful changes has been the way it has affected my relationships. It has helped me deepen my connections with those around me, understand them better, and appreciate their unique gifts. This practice

6. Mark Manson, "One Thing Has the Greatest Impact on Your Life," *Your Next Breakthrough* newsletter, December 26, 2022, https://markmanson.net/breakthrough/002-one-thing-has-the-greatest-impact-on-your-life.

has changed the way I interact with others and the world, allowing me to seek out the good in people and acknowledge their value. It has also encouraged me to look for common threads that connect us. This journey has confirmed that when your relationships improve, your life improves. They are inextricably tied together.

Our bonds with others are so profound, they can be a spiritual practice all on their own—by sharing our energy and essence with another spirit, we create a deep connection that transcends physical and emotional boundaries. Relationships provide a platform to express love, be of service, and provide support to others, empowering us to connect with something greater than ourselves. Through relationships, we can even rise above our everyday, individual selves and connect with higher powers, nature, or humanity as a whole.

We can build a more present, appreciative, and connected life. Therefore, let us invest time and effort into strengthening our relationships through this beautiful practice.

Relationship Strength Training

You can view note-writing as a form of relationship strength training. Just as physical strength training has a transformative effect on your body and mind, relationship strength training can profoundly affect your connections with others. But of course, it doesn't happen all at once. It's more like starting a gym routine in which, at first, you may struggle to lift heavy weights. However, with consistent effort and intention, you'll gradually increase the weight you can handle (capacity) as well as your strength.

I know how this goes. I started powerlifting during the summer of 2023, and my goal was to bench "a plate," which is 135 pounds. When I attempted this for the first time that June, I failed. I was bummed, but it motivated me to keep lifting consistently. I wanted to join the "plate" club and be a "real" lifter. I wasn't scared to put in the work. I just kept showing up, lifting three to four times a week for the next five months. That November I attempted to bench a plate again. To my—and my trainer's—delight, I benched a plate not just once, but twice! I was elated. By holding my intention high and consistently showing up, I reached my goal.

The same principle applies to nurturing relationships. Just as lifting weights strengthens your muscles, putting effort into your relationships strengthens interpersonal bonds. Writing handwritten notes is a type of "heavy lifting" that will, over time, elevate your relationships to a deeper level of connection, understanding, appreciation, and respect. Through intentional practice and commitment to their growth, you'll witness positive results: stronger, more fulfilling relationships.

Long-Distance Relationships

Once upon a time, you spent eight hours a day with your peers in school and after-school activities. In those days, friendships probably came easily. You might have noticed, though, that as you get older, it requires more effort to even maintain, let alone strengthen, your relationships. It's nobody's fault. You and your friends may have simply taken different paths—you might have demanding jobs and more family responsibilities these days.

Or you might just live far from each other—I moved across the country multiple times and left my family and friends behind. It was exciting and scary at the same time. No longer could I drive a few minutes down the road to enjoy a meal with my parents. I was on my own and far away from everything I knew. I missed my hometown, my family, my friends, and my community.

I wanted to stay connected to them in a meaningful way, but walks around the lake with my family and our pups or quick meetups for lunch were no longer options. I had to find another way to stay involved with my people even while I was across the country. Writing handwritten notes gave me a way to stay connected with these dear friends, to share memories, feelings, and appreciation. To keep the flame of friendship alive until we met in person again.

Happily, the road between us goes both ways. I've been delighted to receive notes back from some of these friends. Most recently, postcards arrived from two Burning Man friends I am lucky to see once or twice a year—one from Seattle and one from Miami. I cherish and value our friendships. Our connection makes me smile and warms my heart. That is something I want to keep flourishing, so I will keep writing.

Neighborly Love

I spoke of staying connected from afar, but how about staying connected to those close to you? Who are your neighbors? What kind of neighbor are you? Do you reach out to each other?

When we moved into our home in Austin, our neighbors next door and behind us brought us flowers, champagne, and handwritten notes. These notes gave us warm welcomes into the neighborhood, along with the senders' contact information in case we needed anything. The notes were a way to reach out and extend love in a neighborly way. It was refreshing to know we shared not only lot lines but also, now, a bond. We have continued the practice of exchanging notes, which has helped us slowly but surely build our relationships.

Writing to your neighbors, people you share space and have frequent encounters with, helps you be more active in your community. It can be a quick note, like when I wrote to our apartment neighbor in Miami and thanked him for coming over and being a friendly face down the hall. That's all it takes to acknowledge your neighbors and begin to build community.

The connection you can make with your neighbors is priceless. Recently, we received a note from our neighbor Leslie:

Dear Kristen and Austin,

I wanted to send you both a quick note to thank you for my beautiful flowers for my birthday (and balloon)! Such a treat that really brightened my day. I also want you both to know how grateful I am for your friendship. It has not been the easiest time for me over the last year, and becoming friends with you both has been a joy I was not expecting. Thank you so much again!

Love,

Leslie

Creating an inclusive and loving environment that you want to live in begins with you. This is your opportunity to have an influence on your neighborhood. Take the first step to write your neighbor a handwritten note. Won't you be a friendly neighbor?

Connect Across Generations

You can also use notes to grow relationships with the future by strengthening the bonds between generations. It all starts with kids! By giving a child the gift of receiving their first handwritten note, like I did with my young friend, Blake, you support their journey into the world. You can even write to newborn babies (and their families, of course) to wish them well in this world from the very beginning. I wrote several of these, including:

Welcome to the world, Teddy!

You were blessed with the most loving, caring family . . . and they were blessed with you. Through a long, tumultuous year, you brought joy, excitement, and anticipation. What a gift! You are so loved from near and far. You have admirers (and friends) all the way down in Florida 🙂. I am looking forward to meeting your perfectly new little face.

Love to you and your family,
Kristen

I wrote to people of all ages too:

Elise,

Happy twenty-first birthday to my favorite little sis! I feel like it was just yesterday you were pretending to be a cat, waking me up early from sleepovers to play, and demanding I tickle your feet. What a gift it's been to watch you grow into the woman you are today. You are beautiful on the inside and out. I admire your passion for and love of animals, killer dance moves, and kind heart. Having a sister is like having a built-in best friend and I couldn't ask for a better one.

Cheers to you and your twenty-first year. Dream big, sis . . . the world is yours!

Love you forever,
Kristen

And, of course, Grandma Martha:

Grandma Martha,

Happy happy happy birthday to you! Wow, eighty-nine years young! What a gift it's been to share life with you. I admire your deep faith, commitment to family, and love of life. Thank you for being you. You are loved and appreciated. Wishing you joy, peace, and the best year yet. Cheers to you, Grandma. 🙂

I love you!

Kristen

There is no age limit for pen pals. Whether you're writing to your grandmother or a friend's kids, ask them about what they are up to, give them an update about you, and foster a connection with them from afar.

Reviving Past Relationships

With a handwritten note, you can also rekindle relationships that you treasure, even if the connection has been lost over time. For instance, everyone has "that teacher"—you know, the one who had the greatest impact on your life. My best friend's dad, Randolph, definitely did, and after college graduation, he decided to write to "that teacher" to express his gratitude for helping him discover his love for science.

What started as a simple gesture of appreciation turned into a real-life relationship after a decade of no contact. A pillar of their unique relationship included a creative game of note-writing. It was art in action between two people who had touched each other's lives.

Randolph even attended his teacher's ninetieth birthday party, after which he received a witty note to thank him for showing up. Handwritten notes are a beautiful way to reignite connections and bring people back into your life. Sometimes, they are all it takes to show someone you remember and care.

Building New Relationships

As much as writing notes can strengthen existing relationships, it can also help us create new ones. Yes, I've written handwritten notes to strangers—people I had just met. Just because it is a new person doesn't mean you cannot connect meaningfully.

Some of my "new people" notes have been my favorites. I am tickled to write these notes, which are definitely unexpected. Who writes handwritten notes to their grocery cashier? Or the person stocking the back of the grocery store? To their yoga teacher? To their mail carrier? To their handyperson . . . to the apartment landscaper? Not many, which makes it even more fun.

When we were on vacation in Key West, we had a delightful server. I wrote her a thank-you note. Even if I never saw her again, I wanted to let her know how much she had brightened our morning.

To my surprise, she sent me a postcard back.

Kristen and Austin,
Thank you so much for your kind words. It's so sweet of you! I hope I'll see you soon here at Banana Café.
Warmest regards,
Aksana

These everyday encounters are special and worth recognizing. We are only here for a short while; why not enjoy and appreciate every person we come in contact with and let them know how valued they are? A small surprise of appreciation goes a long way. You can make new connections anywhere. The opportunities are endless, so spread a little love on your path and pick up some friends along the way.

When you meet people and you feel in your bones that you want to cultivate a relationship with them, be honest with that. Do something about it. Take a chance. Write them a note! Investigate, explore, and learn more. Don't let it be the relationship that could have been. Sometimes a friendship can blossom in an unlikely place. Be open to this possibility. And if you feel it, write it.

I've sent and received multiple notes from our realtors in Austin. They know I love writing notes, and they actively practice note-writing as well. Even though we were not physically in Austin, they still reached out to keep in touch. After receiving a cute gift along with a handwritten note from them over the holidays, I realized handwritten notes were a way to validate our relationship. The handwritten notes reminded me that we mattered to them. That our relationship was legitimate, real, and true; even though we were out of sight, we were not out of mind. The steady back-and-forth, pen pal–type communication confirmed that we both thought the relationship was worthwhile.

Why not give people this type of heartful validation? It feels good. It makes you feel a deeper connection with the note sender and the world in general. Writing handwritten notes gives you a sense of belonging and reassurance that you are an important member of your community, big or small. We all want to belong. To know we are interconnected with something greater than ourselves.

Chapter Four:

Creating Joy

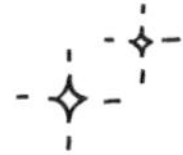

"I am going to spend as much time as I can creating delightful things out of my existence because that's what brings me awake and that's what brings me alive."

—Elizabeth Gilbert, *Big Magic*

I have asked and continue to ask myself: Do I want to be a creator or a consumer? Realistically, humans will be both, but we can deliberately choose which way the pendulum swings. As I've personally experienced, creating is life-giving—joy-giving—and consuming is life-taking. Many of my notes were written to celebrate the joy that others create on a daily basis, such as this one to a butterfly keeper at the Key West butterfly exhibit:

Alex,

Thank you for talking to us about the turacos. We loved learning their names, personalities, and backgrounds. Interacting with Andora, Maurice, and JJ was the absolute best. Thank you for sharing your passion and love for these beautiful creatures. It was cool how the butterflies would fly around you as you walked. Thanks for sharing the

magic with us. We had such a special time at the Butterfly and Nature Conservatory. It truly took my breath away.
With deep gratitude,
Kristen Tremonti and Austin Reiter

Creating lights me up. It expands me. Consuming, not so much. I've overconsumed my fair share of social media, clothes, food—you name it. Even while creating, I am not above getting lost in doomscrolls or losing a stunning number of hours on Instagram. Hours I will never get back. Hours when inspiration stopped and I became stuck in media quicksand, that dark soul-sucking hole of *I'm not good enough or far enough along or pretty enough* or *I don't take cool enough vacations* or *my clothes suck*. Overconsuming doesn't fill me up, it makes me feel shitty.

I never feel shitty after writing a note. It's like when you complete a workout you didn't want to start—you always feel better once it's over. I'm still a consumer and my attention still gets lost, but I know there is a better way to spend my time. Writing a note takes more effort than doomscrolling, but the rewards are life-giving and limitless! You could get your dream house, receive an email from a favorite author, connect with old friends, make someone cry tears of joy, make someone feel less alone, or put a smile on someone's face. These are all miracles to me.

Constant Creativity

If I am writing notes, I know I am creating and putting some of myself, my love, into the world. I discover joy every time I create one of these meaningful messages. Creating makes me feel good. It feels like I am harnessing the magic within me to create more magic. It fills me up with the good stuff.

With this practice, my creativity, which had long been silent, is now being put to use. My creative muscles are being exercised. By doodling balloons on the front of my notes, drawing a party hat on my dog, or sending hummingbird stickers to surprise a recipient, I've found new ways to make my notes special and fun! I am making space for inspiration to shine through. As Steven Pressfield says, "the professional doesn't wait for inspiration, she acts in anticipation of its apparition."[7]

Collaborating with my creativity and inspiration feels good; scratching my creative itch is both satisfying and rewarding. By practicing creativity, I've opened the floodgates to more creativity. I've become an explorer of ideas.

Instead of finding cards to send to people, I've realized I can create my own stationery and send out my own cards! These cards might have my dog on the front with a note in his mouth. The back could include my favorite lovingkindness mantra. My ideas have been going wild, and I am loving it! I feel like I used to feel in art class when I'm making something new—out there in the unknown, not sure of what I might create, until it becomes something tangible that I am proud of. I enjoy flexing my creative muscles. Stretching my abilities. Expressing my silly, fun inside to the outside too.

I've had so much fun expressing my creative side. I am not alone in this; nurturing our creativity has been shown to have a significant positive impact on overall well-being. By engaging in creative activities, we connect with our authentic selves and facilitate healing in our nervous systems. According to *Forbes*, engaging in creative practices can reduce anxiety, depression, and stress, and even aid in processing trauma.[8] Research has demonstrated that expressive writing in particular can help

---

7. Steven Pressfield, *The War of Art* (Black Irish Entertainment LLC, 2002).
8. Ashley Stahl, "Here's How Creativity Actually Improves Your Health," *Forbes*, July 25, 2018, https://www.forbes.com/sites/ashleystahl/2018/07/25/heres-how-creativity-actually-improves-your-health/.

individuals effectively manage negative emotions.[9] In addition to the psychological benefits, creative pursuits can also offer improved brain function and physical health.

Engaging in creative activities has been shown to increase happiness, reduce the risk of developing dementia, improve mental health by boosting focus and releasing dopamine, enhance immune function, and promote greater cognitive integration between the left and right hemispheres of the brain.[10] Creativity is fundamental to human existence.

That's a peek at the science of creativity, and the evidence is compelling. But there's more; let's not lose sight of the magical side.

Radical Amazement

It's all too easy to get lost in the busyness of life and forget to appreciate the wonder and magic of the world around us, but it's there. Through note-writing, we can tap back into the amazing that is constantly surrounding us.

"Radical amazement" is a term used by the Jewish philosopher Rabbi Abraham Joshua Heschel to describe a deep sense of wonder and awe in the face of the mysteries of existence.[11] It suggests a willingness to be surprised and amazed by the world, to remain open to the possibility of encountering the divine or the transcendent in everyday experiences.

---

9. Deborah Siegel-Acevedo, "Writing Can Help Us Heal from Trauma," *Harvard Business Review* July 1, 2021, https://hbr.org/2021/07/writing-can-help-us-heal-from-trauma.

10. Ashley Stahl, "Here's How Creativity Actually Improves Your Health," *Forbes*, July 25, 2018, https://www.forbes.com/sites/ashleystahl/2018/07/25/heres-how-creativity-actually-improves-your-health/.

11. Rabbi Abraham Joshua Heschel, "Radical Amazement," *Awakin.org*, accessed April 1, 2025, https://www.awakin.org/v2/read/view.php?tid=1080.

Sometimes I lose track of those experiences. I get disconnected from myself, the world, and nature. Lost as to my purpose, operating without direction. Lost on the internet, where I surrender my attention to the void of unimportance—the scroll hole. I forget to stay present in the wonder and awesomeness that is life. I forget to rejoice in the fact that I'm having a human experience with all these other humans.

I don't have time to forget that. None of us does. Oliver Burkeman says the typical human life is on average four thousand weeks. I don't want to waste any more of my minutes unconsciously lost.

Through note-writing, I'm able to find my way back. I tap back into the wonders that are constantly surrounding me. I get to listen to the man sharing his piano-playing skills at the Kawasaki store, soak in the experience, and honor it and its magic by thanking him for brightening my day. Or to a restaurant server sharing his spiritual findings. I get to learn more about his life and thank him for sharing what inspires him.

I write notes to these people because it helps me remember the beauty all around me. It helps me recognize the loving people and moments I encounter every day. The humans who appear in our life experience present us with unique gifts and never-ending lessons, but only if we are present and open enough to experience them. To consciously recognize what we are constantly given.

Too often, we miss that opportunity. Believe me, I've been there more often than I like to admit. On a "lost" day or in a "lost" moment—maybe after spending too much time on my phone or just in my own head—I have regularly missed these magical everyday opportunities to connect to others and see the good in the world. To learn from someone. And I didn't even realize what I was missing.

Instead, by writing a note, I can seize the moment, giving it the respect it deserves. Note-writing helps me thank others for playing their part, for enriching this radically amazing life. By taking the time to recognize and honor the kindness and beauty in the people and moments we encounter every day, we can all practice radical amazement.

Stubborn Gladness

Some days it's harder to walk in the glow of the amazing than others, of course. Fortunately, we can reinforce our radical amazement practice with the application of "stubborn gladness." Stubborn gladness is a term coined by the poet Jack Gilbert, who wrote about the importance of persistently seeking out joy and beauty in the world, even in the face of difficulty and pain. It suggests a kind of determined optimism, a refusal to let the darkness of the world overwhelm one's ability to experience and appreciate moments of happiness and beauty.[12]

This practice takes work. We must be persistent in our efforts to notice the constant gifts in our lives—the subtle joys that exist within ordinary moments. It is in these moments, the ones we might overlook unless we are determined to seek and find them, that we discover the beauty of life. Remember to find pleasure in the mundane and cherish the simple things—from the heartfelt care of the veterinarian and vet assistants who make your dog's nail-trim experience less traumatizing, to the jolly conversation offered by the UPS worker helping you ship a package, to the kind words from a neighbor on your daily walk.

Note-writing can help us redirect our attention from distractions and numbing activities to purposeful observation;

12. Jack Gilbert, "A Brief for the Defense," *Collected Poems*, Alfred A. Knopf, 2012.

in other words, we can train ourselves to practice stubborn gladness. Armed with nothing but paper and pen, we can learn to look inside ourselves and our surroundings to appreciate the people and things around us. We can ask ourselves more often: Who can I uplift today? What can I appreciate? What can I write about? What can I dig deeper into?

My intention for asking these questions and writing these notes is to transform life's difficulties and uncertainties into moments of appreciation. Rather than being consumed by the unknown, I choose to focus on the goodness that surrounds us every day. Daily practice requires a conscious decision to combat life's trials—our handwritten notes are our high road to appreciation.

Right about now, you may be asking yourself a question: Can something as simple as note-writing really create a paradigm shift that replaces fear with gratitude and stubborn gladness? That's my intention, and I think it's possible—through persistent efforts to notice and delight in everyday moments—to weave our magic spells of words and cast goodness and love to note receivers.

And truly, why not try? We can at least brighten our days and the days of those around us, spreading joy and positivity through the simple act of appreciation.

Chapter Five:

Living Gratitude

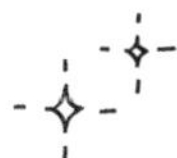

"Without gratitude what is the point of seeing, and without seeing what is the object of gratitude?"

—Epictetus, Discourses, 1.6 1–2, *The Daily Stoic*

My twenty-fifth note was to an old boss. We had a complicated relationship. By complicated, I mean she was infamously hard to work with. My coworker coined her an "emotional terrorist." During my time working on her team, I cried frequently, worked with deep fear, and developed an autoimmune disease. My body and mind were searching for safe havens. Looking back, I realize I could have given myself that mental shelter. At that time, though, I did not have the necessary tools. Instead, my friend and I would sneak away to the back closet and discuss and cry about the latest dramatic happenings. I was stressed, and it was physically wreaking havoc on my body. I was mentally unwell, and it showed on the outside.

A note to that former boss:

Thank you for mentoring me. I appreciate the countless hours you took to explain new terms, share market knowledge, discuss ideas, and connect me with people in the business. You helped me navigate through an industry dominated by men and showed me how to find success as a woman. I remember my first pitch. My hand was shaking while holding my pen, and afterward you encouragingly said, "It's OK to shake, just don't drop it." You exemplified bravery and encouraged me to step up to challenges. You influenced numerous aspects of my work by demonstrating such excellent presentation skills and giving me tools I still use today. I am grateful for the time and energy you put into teaching me. I admire your toughness, leadership, confidence, expertise, work ethic, and sense of humor. Thank you for believing in me even when it and I were challenging. These words are not enough to thank you for what you have given and done for me, although it is a small start. Thank you. Wishing you continued success in work and in life.

Respectfully,
Kristen

It took a long time for me to be able to write this note. Even after this woman physically left our company, I still held on to my anger. I just couldn't let it go. I wondered what I had done to deserve that kind of treatment and disrespect. It felt unfair. I felt wronged. In hindsight, I see I was stuck in a classic victim mindset, carrying around unhealed emotions and traumas. It completely depleted my energy, but I held on to my trauma like a badge of honor. I didn't want to admit it was still an issue or dig further into my emotions. I couldn't thrive until I did, but at the time, I was focused on simply surviving.

We remained in the same industry, so I continued to hear her name every so often. Sure, the pain had dulled, but I still felt it. I wanted to be free. I finally realized I had to change the story, if not for her, then for me. I would write her a note.

I had to step back and widen my perspective and acknowledge that she was saddled with her own responsibilities, stress, and problems. After all, I believe—and preach—that everyone is doing their best with what they have, and that had to include her too. I also knew that my negative thoughts and emotions weren't helping either of us. Instead of focusing my attention there, I decided I would pinpoint her positive attributes and articulate how she had contributed to my growth. I would thank her for it.

It took the laser focus of writing this note for me to find the goodness in our relationship. To my surprise, I realized how much I had to be grateful for with this woman. I had received lessons, guidance, and support from her. And we had shared laughs, mutual progress, and teamwork. We actually accomplished a lot together. Seeing all of that written down, I felt like a weight was lifted off me.

I'm so glad I wrote that note and sent it. For both of us. She didn't personally acknowledge the note, but a ripple of energy came from it, nonetheless. Months after I sent the note, she recommended me to her friend in the business for a job opening. This was completely unexpected and heartwarming.

Hearing from her friend that she spoke highly of me and had recommended me for this role made me feel both happy and relieved. I hope my note helped her understand my appreciation for her role in my development and professional life. The note helped me shift my perspective on our relationship from a victim mindset into an empowered mindset. Instead of seeing myself as the victim of an emotional terrorist, I saw an opportunity to learn and grow.

You can write your own note of forgiveness. Write it to whatever emotional baggage you are holding on to. To whatever relationship has been haunting you. I chose to send my note because it felt right for me, but you don't have to physically send out the note to experience the benefits of healing. You can throw the note away or even light it on fire. The point is to write it down, to work through it, to put your feelings into words. To get what is on the inside out. To release whatever is stuck inside there. Not for them, but for you, so you can heal and move forward. By processing what happened, you can begin to make sense of your feelings, and you have an opportunity to flip the narrative. To change the story. You owe this to yourself. No one can help you with this, not even me. You have to do it for yourself. Write the note.

Before I started this note-writing journey, my gratitude practice was not alive. It was something I felt on the inside but didn't fully express. I might have thought briefly about things I was grateful for, but then I'd move on without taking action.

I knew it was worth doing because there is plenty of proof out there that gratitude can deeply transform the body and mind. Study after study consistently shows that gratitude is correlated with fewer symptoms of illness, more optimism and happiness, stronger relationships, and more generous behavior.[13] In his Daily Gratitude Booster meditation, Matthew Hepburn, a meditation teacher on the Ten Percent Happier app (now renamed as Happier), says gratitude builds hope in hard times, lowers stress hormones, and is the single best predictor of emotional well-being and healthy relationships.[14] According to the Mindfulness Awareness Research

---

13. Summer Allen, PhD, "The Science of Gratitude," *Greater Good Science Center.* (2018): 28-40, https://ggsc.berkeley.edu/images/uploads/GGSC-JTF_White_Paper-Gratitude-FINAL.pdf.

14. Matthew Hepburn, "Daily Gratitude Booster," Ten Percent Happier App, 2023, https://podscripts.co/podcasts/ten-percent-happier-with-dan-harris/the-massive-power-of-not-taking-sht-for-granted-bonus-meditation-with-matthew-hepburn.

Center of UCLA, regularly expressing gratitude "changes the molecular structure of the brain."[15]

Meanwhile, I was ignoring all of this evidence and doing the opposite of living in gratitude. I was living in a constant state of stress and victimhood. Is it any wonder that this was when I first developed my autoimmune disease, psoriasis? There were red patches all over my face and body. One time my cheeks turned bright red from trying a new skin product. Not only did it feel like my face was on fire but it itched like crazy. I was supposed to go out that night but instead stayed home, in tears. I was too embarrassed of my appearance and was physically struggling with my skin. My skin was living proof of the unwellness that was going on internally, not because of this woman's behaviors but because of my responses and reactions to her.

Fortunately, I haven't experienced physical symptoms of this disease in many years, and I owe this to serious lifestyle and health changes. This includes an active gratitude practice. I am a healthier, happier person on the inside and the outside because I changed my internal world. When I finally took action by writing handwritten notes and sending them out into the world, I brought my gratitude practice to life.

Through gratitude, by recognizing what you do have, you are able to amplify your blessings. Blessings, turn up! All it takes is intentional focus sprinkled with appreciation.

15. Joan Moran, "Pause, reflect and give thanks: the power of gratitude during the holidays," UCLA: Newsroom, October 29, 2013, https://newsroom.ucla.edu/stories/gratitude-249167.

Paying Attention

"Thrives with attention."

That's the phrase I found when I was looking into personality traits of my dog's breed, the American Staffordshire Terrier. Austin and I laughed reading this, because it rings true. Our dog loves it when people talk to him, admire him, play with him, and make him feel included. He loves to participate in activities together like going on walks. He likes to be invited to ride in the car together. It got me thinking—don't we all thrive with the right type of attention?

But what, exactly, is attention? Attention is being with something fully, focusing without trying to change it. According to Dictionary.com, attention is "notice taken of someone or something; the regarding of someone or something as interesting or important."

Gratitude practice is powerful because it helps us focus—to pay attention—and we need the help. Have you ever driven somewhere and gotten there and seemed to have missed the whole drive? Me too. And this can happen at any time in our daily lives; as a result, we miss out on our own reality, the small parts that make up the whole. Through gratitude we can zoom out, witnessing our reality from a distance. And we can zoom in on the details of our object of gratitude, increasing our awareness through a larger and smaller lens of appreciation.

Paying attention is an act of lovingkindness toward ourselves and others. It allows us to build self-awareness, which helps us get back in touch with ourselves. Paying attention allows us to feel what our bodies and emotions are communicating at a deeper level. In fact, attention has direct physiological results.

"Attention is like a spotlight, and what it illuminates streams into your mind and shapes your brain," says Rick Hanson in his book *Buddha's Brain: The Practical Neuroscience of Happiness, Love, and Wisdom*. The things we pay attention to are literally the building blocks of our brain tissue. Our neurons wire in response to what we focus upon. What you pay attention to grows. Let's be honest, what have we been paying attention to? Where has our attention been going?

Where *should* it be going? As Gretchen Rubin writes in *The Happiness Project*, "Any single happy experience may be amplified or minimized depending on how much attention you give it." Attention is opportunity. Through handwritten notes, you can amplify every positive experience no matter how big or small. You can write about it, reminisce on the details, the sensations, the feelings. You can make the experience bigger through intentional recall. Through note-writing, you can give your full attention to the note recipient. You can take notice of their strengths and the good that moves through them. You can show genuine interest in them by focusing on how they enrich your life and the world. You can share their importance to you. You can appreciate them being exactly who they are. By noticing and appreciating the good, you can help people feel more positive emotions, such as joy and pleasure.

The more we practice, the more we change on the inside. The more we feel at ease, the more connected we are and the more joyful we become. With practice, we get better at recognizing that every day is a miracle, that our life is a gift, and that love is abundant and all around us.

I noticed this when we were living in Miami, and our dishwasher was broken. A handy person stopped by our apartment. He joyfully hummed songs while he worked. I was taken aback by his joy—and it immediately improved my day and made me smile. I sent him a note to thank him, and I told him how he had brightened my day. I realized that by writing these notes, I was stopping to recognize the good. His joy was contagious. It spread to me, filling me with abundance and love that I was committed to passing along to others.

Through my note-writing, I started interacting with people in my life in a deeper way. Instead of letting the small details pass me by, I listened for them, and I acknowledged them. Instead of scrolling on my phone, I was giving people and their lives the attention they deserved. I celebrated with them, and it made the world seem like a brighter place. One that I truly enjoyed living and participating in.

Appreciation is the highest form of gratitude. When we recognize the little things, they become big things.

Gratitude in Action

So, are you ready to show up as a grateful person? What does this grateful person do? How does this grateful person act? Well, let's start with how they *shouldn't* act, with an embarrassing scene from my twenties, when I received a flower arrangement as a birthday present from an ex-boyfriend's mom. I was terrified of her. She wasn't mean per se, but she was a boss and *the* boss. She intimidated me. But she gave me a beautiful flower arrangement, and I felt sincere gratitude for it. It was a thoughtful gift.

She gave me the arrangement while I was at their house, and when I left, I forgot to take it with me. *I left the gift behind.* What an idiot. I can't think of a worse way to show you are grateful for something. Ugh. Back then I wasn't writing thank-you notes. I was too busy worrying about the next party or social gathering or my boyfriend. Or succumbing to the anxiety of wanting my ex-boyfriend's mom to like me.

The lesson here: To receive the full healing benefits of gratitude, we must put it into action. The most valuable gratitude isn't just a feeling, it's an action. Studies show that displays of gratitude are more valuable than solely feeling gratitude toward others.[16] That may be why writing handwritten notes feels transformative—it lets you turn your gratitude into something physical. Hand-writing notes is an excellent way to cultivate gratitude because it's a physical display and active expression of your appreciation.

Practicing gratitude is a foundational step for improving happiness. And who doesn't want to be happier? According to Dr. Mark Hyman, practicing gratitude improves psychological health by reducing toxic emotions like envy and regret.[17] Practicing gratitude wires and fires new neural connections and enhances dopamine production.

As Robert Emmons puts it, "Gratitude makes us appreciate the value of something, and when we appreciate the value of something, we extract more benefits from it; we're less likely to take it for granted. . . . With gratitude we become greater participants in our lives as opposed to spectators."[18]

When I received that gift of flowers, I was trying so hard to be liked and accepted that it got in the way of me being myself. I felt shitty for forgetting, and I never wrote a thank-you note. If I had known what I know now, I might still have forgotten the flowers. Shit happens. Although I probably would have written a thank-you note. It may or may not have gotten her to like me. But it would have probably gotten me to like myself more. Since then, I've leveled up my habits. Not all of them, but definitely the note-writing ones.

---

16. Nathaniel M. Lambert, Margaret S. Clark, Jared Durtschi, Frank D. Fincham, and Steven M. Graham, "Benefits of Expressing Gratitude: Expressing Gratitude to a Partner Changes One's View of the Relationship," *Psychological Science* 21, no. 4 (2010): 574–580.

17. Mark Hyman, "Gratitude Heals," *DrHyman.com*, 2018, https://drhyman.com/blog/2018/12/04/gratitude-heals/.

18. Robert Emmons, "Why Gratitude Is Good," *Greater Good Magazine*, November 16, 2010.

What I've learned from this is that we must make time for and pay attention to the things that are important to us. And act accordingly. Our actions tell the story. What habits do you have that could be replaced with better ones? Is there time that would be better spent doing the heartwarming, feel-good work of note-writing?

Chapter Six:

Sharing Our Gifts

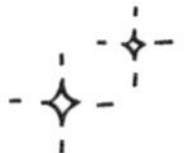

"Feeling gratitude and not expressing it is like wrapping a present and not giving it."

—William Arthur Ward

During my year of notes, I wrote two heartfelt messages to my Grandma Margaret. One was a surprise note I sent while I was away in Miami, and the other was for her ninety-second birthday, which fell on Mother's Day. I wanted to express how much she meant to me and how much I cherished our relationship. It was important to me to share my words and feelings with her while she was still alive, and I am grateful that I did.

Grandma Margaret,

Happy birthday and Grandmother's Day, Grandma! I am beyond grateful to have you in my life. I appreciate your never-ending kindness, genuine interest, and love. I've always enjoyed spending time with you, from shopping to phone calls to just sitting around catching up. I cherish our relationship and all of our memories together. Thanks

for making me feel special and loved. Wishing you the best year yet. Cheers to you and #92!
I love you,
Kristen

Sadly, she passed away shortly after. Although I felt immense sadness and grief, I found comfort in knowing that I had expressed my love and appreciation for her through those notes. Writing those messages to her was one of the best decisions I've ever made, and the handwritten notes served as a tangible reminder of our relationship that was literally sealed with love. Those notes were gifts to us both.

Handwritten notes are true gifts to be shared, not treasures to be hoarded. The dictionary definition of treasure is to keep something valuable or valued carefully. A gift, on the other hand, is something given willingly to someone without payment—a present. Handwritten notes are gifts that can be held, reread, and revisited for years to come, serving as a tangible reminder of the relationship between the giver and the recipient.

I understood the power of this gift deeply when a family friend, who had fought hard against melanoma, ultimately lost the battle. He left behind a wife and four sons. However, he didn't leave them empty-handed. He left handwritten notes for each of their milestone moments in life. He wrote notes for their weddings, certain birthdays, and other important events. These notes allowed his presence to be felt and his voice to be heard even though he wasn't physically there. The notes were a way for him to continue to be a part of their lives, even after his passing. His words carried his spirit and kept his connection with his family alive. The value of these handwritten notes is immeasurable. They are worth more than gold, and they will be treasured forever.

Meaningful Gifts That Keep Giving

Humans don't live forever, but we can keep our memories and love alive through handwritten notes. These notes can serve as a "photo album" of scenes created with words that capture our thoughts, feelings, and experiences. When we pay attention to the small details and moments and physically record them, we can freeze them in time and share them with others. These notes can bring us joy and comfort, reminding us that we are loved. Years later, you can pull one out of a drawer and open the floodgates of feelings past.

I write notes to keep my own memories alive. Reflecting on them and remembering the small details brings a smile to my face. Writing notes also gives me and the receiver the opportunity to reminisce about the past, nostalgically recalling our shared experiences. When someone reaches out to me about receiving their note, I immediately pull up my copies—yes, these notes are so precious to me that I always document them—so I can see what I wrote, the specifics of the card, and the little details. This heightens the memory and helps me feel in tune with the receiver. Reminiscing about the goodness together makes a special moment, a celebration of our connection, and an opportunity to feel joy. These notes—both the ones you receive and the ones you send—are your special gifts.

You don't have to be rich to give someone a meaningful gift. That's fortunate because the high cost of living is a harsh reality we all face. If you are living in the world today, you have felt the pain of inflation, as the price of goods and services has skyrocketed. Unfortunately, throughout my note-writing year, my paychecks did not keep pace. My earnings were less than half of what they had been when I was settled in Kansas City. While we traveled wherever football took us, I simply didn't have the funds for gifting as much as I had been accustomed to in the past. This was a hard pill for me to swallow. I still had the itch to give, but how would I do it when I was struggling to pay my never-ending bills?

Happily, I found a way to give that didn't require bankrupting myself. Instead of wallowing in guilt or inadequacy, I transformed my problem into a heartfelt, creative solution by gifting handwritten notes.

Sure, handwritten notes aren't completely cost-free, but they offer a big bang for your buck. Magic-word spells can be held on to, cherished, displayed on the refrigerator, and reflected upon as a reminder of love, support, and appreciation. A handwritten note is more of a present than metals, jewels, and gems. And it is rare, especially in the modern world—a one-of-a-kind gift of human connection.

You can create this magic for almost nothing. And you can deliver it in the most magical way—through the post office! I'm not kidding. Consider the journey your note will go on. From a mailbox or blue collection box, your letter is collected by postal carriers and brought to the community post office. Next, it's off to the process plant for sorting. Here, the mail is sorted by destination. The note is transported to the recipient's local post office or sorting facility. This can be done by road, rail, air, or sea.

Finally, the mail is delivered to the recipient's home by a postal carrier who arrives on foot or by bicycle, motorcycle, or car, depending on the distance and volume of the mail. This process can take days or weeks. Your note is a well-traveled piece of magic that has floated through the world from the sender to the receiver.

Open the mailbox and discover an unexpected gift: a handwritten note full of love; words that were written just for you. It's magic. A woman in one of my note-writing workshops talked passionately about just such a moment, when her daughter received her first real letter in the mail. A message intended and specifically crafted for her was sitting in the mailbox! It lit up her little world.

Yes, magic.

The Gift of Nurturing

Writing a heartfelt note is all about nurturing and nourishing our human relationships. Just as plants respond to fertilizer, humans respond to positive energy and recognition, so give the gift of nurturing—the gift of TLC. Writing a handwritten note is a way to provide the little bit of extra care needed to set someone off in the right direction. To lift them closer to the sun and jump-start their growth.

People grow and flourish best in an atmosphere of awe—surrounded by love and appreciation and recognition. We want to feel loved, appreciated, and recognized for our beauty and beingness. Let's continue to nurture our humans and watch them grow. With the right care, attention, and support, we can all flourish and thrive. We are meant to look after each other and give what we can to help. It's the little things like a heartfelt note that can make all the difference.

For example, I truly admire the positive energy my favorite music artist, Griz, is putting into the world, and I thought he deserved some recognition. Here's a note I wrote to him:

> *Griz,*
>
> *Thank you for being you. Your music is incredible . . . literally my number one. I jam so hard in my car (pretend concerts) to your songs, especially "Juicy" and "Vibe Check." You keep releasing bangers! Even better than your music (is that possible?!) is your message. The way you preach inclusivity, love, and respect in life and at your shows is inspirational. Thank you for using your platform for the greater good. You are the funky, authentic, radical*

hero the world needed. Thank you for your energy. Your vibes are unmatched. Keep doing you, groove king! You're changing the world!

Peace, love, and gratitude,
Kristen Tremonti

The Gift of Appreciation

As Mister Rogers says, "As human beings, our job in life is to help people realize how rare and valuable each one of us really is, that each of us has something that no one else has—or ever will have—something inside that is unique to all time."[19]

You can build people up by pointing out their greatest assets. Writing notes has helped me recognize what is special about every note receiver. Crafting with words the way they make me feel, what I admire about them, what unique gifts they possess, and how they inspire me, I can celebrate their value. With words, I can specifically call out what makes them wonderful. With words, I can appreciate and love them for who they are.

Lynette,

Thank you for your ongoing support and friendship. I appreciate your listening ears and warm, understanding heart. In a world full of constant change, you make me feel grounded. Thank you for holding space for me through the wild ride that is life. I'm forever working on your therapist's advice of sitting with my feelings 🙂. *You are an important and special person to me. I am consistently inspired by your growth, expansion, and good energy. My appreciation for you is endless. Love and miss you dearly.*

Bacon and aliens 4ever,
Kristen

---

19. Fred Rogers, *The World According to Mister Rogers: Important Things to Remember* (Hachette Books, 2019), 105.

The Gift of Comfort

"When times are hard, we need a deep kind of comfort," writes Matt Haig in *The Comfort Book*. "Something elemental. A solid support. A rock to hold on to. The kind we already have inside us. But which we sometimes need a bit of help to see."

During times of turmoil, we can be a source of comfort for others. You never know exactly what someone is going through. Everyone is dealing with their own shit. No one is exempt from the highs and lows of life. That was made clear during the COVID epidemic. No one was "safe" or unaffected.

When I receive a handwritten note, it instantly brightens my day. It's a small act of kindness, though it provides a significant amount of warmth. Through handwritten notes we can help others find the good in themselves by shining a light on it. We can remind them there is always light around them and inside them. Although we cannot stop their suffering, we can provide comfort. We can help others see there is still good.

> *Annie,*
>
> *My heart is with you as you mourn the loss of Nana and your Uncle Mason. I am sorry you have to experience this sadness. I hope you are able to find some peace and comfort together with your family as you remember their lives and all the lives they've touched. I am here to lean on whenever you need some extra support.*
>
> *Sending you a big hug and all my love,*
> *Kristen*

The Gift of Celebration

Handwritten notes give us an opportunity to celebrate others. To take part in their triumphs and successes. To get a taste of what it's like to be in their world. To share in the joy. Celebrating others can bring a sense of fulfillment and happiness that cannot be achieved through self-centered pursuits. So take the time to celebrate others and find happiness along the way.

Austin,

Congratulations, my Saint! I am over-the-moon excited for you and your new team. What an awesome opportunity for you to shine and show them your greatness! I am in constant awe of your hard work, commitment, discipline, and drive. I admire your mental and physical toughness. You face challenges head-on with true courage. You are unbelievably skilled with unmatched awareness. You lead by example and are always looking to improve and be your best self. I am beaming with pride 🙂. You deserve all the success and happiness life has to offer. Go get what's yours. "Be so good they can't ignore you." YEAR 7 BB LFG!!!

I love you,
Kristen

According to philosopher John Stuart Mill, "Those are only happy who have their minds fixed on some object other than their own happiness; on the happiness of others, on the improvement of mankind . . . some art or pursuit, followed not as a means, but . . . an ideal end. Aiming this at something else, they find happiness by the way."[20]

The Gift of Reflection

Just as butterflies can't see their own wings, some people can't see their own beauty. Some are unable to recognize how far they've come, how much they've evolved, grown, and

---

20. John Stuart Mill, *The Classic Autobiography of John Stuart Mill* (Liberal Arts Press, 1957).

flourished. Here lies an opportunity for you to be a mirror of their goodness.

By reflecting what you see, you can shine their light back on them. If you see something special in someone, let them know. Sometimes we all get lost and need others to remind us of our goodness. You have the opportunity to recognize and acknowledge their special importance to the world.

As Jaiya John writes in *Daughter Drink This Water*, "If you see someone who has good light, thank them for it. It will help them keep the light on."

Christine,

Thank you for your positive attitude and spirit. I enjoyed talking to you about where we've been and the vibe of cities. You are interesting, helpful, and kind. Your goodness shines through you, even behind a mask 🙂. *Thank you for bringing joy to my self-care spa day. Meeting you was such a treat! Wishing you continued success and joy wherever you go.*

With love and respect,
Kristen Tremonti

Receiving Gifts in Return

I frequently receive appreciative replies to my handwritten notes, and that means a lot to me. Mostly I receive handwritten notes in return, sometimes postcards, and someone once gave me a Starbucks gift card and a travel cup. The most unique gift I got in return was a butterfly milkweed seed.

Many recipients share that their hearts were touched. That they cried. Someone shared that my note is on their refrigerator.

I love getting replies like this one, from one of my past yoga teachers (the milkweed seed giver):

Sweet Kristen,

Your beautiful card made me teary-eyed. I love the concept of your project and can't wait to watch it unfold. You're such an inspirational ray of light. Thanks for continually polishing your diamond and shining so brightly. Here's to not leaving things unsaid.

So much love,

Jen

There were multiple notes that arrived "at just the right time." One note was returned, and I had to send it back—on the second try, it miraculously arrived on the receiver's birthday. It seemed that the universe's timing was working out just the way it was supposed to, beautifully designed. I wrote to an event creator, who wrote me back and said, "Thank you *so much* for the card. It brought me tears of joy. Sometimes I wonder if I'm reaching anyone, so I appreciate your sweet note of support." I had another kind soul reply, "What did I do to deserve this?!"

This kind of feedback happens to pretty much everyone who sends handwritten notes. A woman in one of my workshops wrote me a handwritten note and said the reactions she'd received from the cards she'd sent were proof of how important it is to give that gift. She wrote a note to her dad and said he has brought it up every time she's seen him since—not even with words, just a look followed by a big hug.

Another woman in a workshop wrote back to me: "I've already heard back from the person who had lost her husband and had written a motivational book to help others. She was so moved that I had taken the time to send her a card that it made her cry."

I gave Mike, our fitness trainer in Sarasota, his note in person after our workout. He read it while Austin and I were still there, which I did not expect. The smile on his face was one I had never seen before. It was pure joy.

Austin says receiving a handwritten note is like a hug with words. There is just nothing like it. It is transferring your energy and emotions into a physical output. A word hug.

You never know how you are going to touch someone's life with a handwritten note, and part of its beauty is the mystery that you will never know the full impact. When you give a gift, you might receive another or greater gift in return.

Timeless Gifts

A handwritten note is a gift that outlasts the moment. A note can capture a moment in time, freeze an emotion, and preserve a connection. Your words can help you save a snapshot of your feelings, your expression, past events, and shared history—gifts to be kept and reread on a rainy day, offering comfort, solace, and joy.

We all have people in our lives who have touched us in meaningful ways. They have been our mentors, our friends, our confidants, and our family. Let us take the time to express our love and gratitude to them through handwritten notes. Let us leave behind a legacy of our spirit, our essence, and our love.

Our time on Earth is finite. We cannot purchase more of it, nor can we trade it in for anything else. As such, time is arguably the most valuable resource we possess, and there is no greater gift we can give to others than our time. Going the extra mile, investing additional effort, and taking the time to express our affection through a handwritten note is a priceless gesture.

In today's fast-paced world, we strive to "save time" by reducing human interaction and connection. When we eliminate the possibility of connection, we aren't gaining anything. Instead, we are missing out on gifts we might have shared.

These gifts can last lifetimes. They are heirlooms through which we can pass the essence of our spirit down through the generations.

Chapter Seven:

Transforming Ourselves

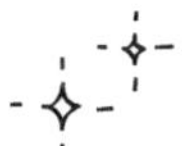

"Don't ask the world to change—you change first. Then you'll get a good enough look at the world so that you'll be able to change whatever you think ought to be changed."

—Anthony De Mello, *Awareness*

Through that year of note-writing, I found my voice. I gained the skill of expressing myself and my truth more clearly. I learned to harness my feelings and emotions on the inside and share them on the outside. I practiced how to create something from nothing, to trust my intuition and speak it aloud. I built confidence in myself and my abilities. I practiced opening my heart. I practiced vulnerability. I practiced persevering through mental and physical challenges. From getting up and out of bed in the morning to taking care of myself to keeping a positive attitude through the "limbo times" and multiple moves. I kept the promise to myself to write a note every day, and in doing so I built trust in myself. This increased my confidence. I gained a new perspective on the world and how I could contribute. I stepped into the role of showing up for myself and for others every day in a creative, thoughtful, intentional, and meaningful way. I transformed myself and my life.

A huge part of that transformation was that I was better able to connect with people I loved and share that love. When my grandmother passed away at age ninety-two, shortly after I had written my 365th note, I was able to write a eulogy and speak at her funeral. Two years earlier, that would have felt impossible. I wouldn't have been able to find the words to represent the feelings in my heart. But because of my note-writing practice, I was able to reflect deeply on our relationship and her light and to capture in words my experience of her essence.

I took a deep breath and started reading the words I had written in her honor:

> *My heart hurts knowing I will never see my grandma again in the flesh, although I know she will live on within me and all who loved her. I will see her in the trees and the squirrels she loved to watch. I will feel her warmth and kindness. Her love will always remain.*
>
> *Grandma Margaret was sensitive and felt deeply. This is one of the reasons why our relationship was so special. Our spirits connected. There was true appreciation between us. The purest kind. She was my soul friend. There wasn't a conversation we had that we didn't tell each other, "I love you."*
>
> *She was proud of everything I did. She was "tickled" by the places I would visit and the things I would do. It made me feel good that she enjoyed hearing about and took interest in my adventures, and I was always eager to share them with her. She made me feel like the most special person in the world.*
>
> *She loved her family. She was delighted to receive a call or a visit. She would light up with joy. I have many mem-*

ories looking through her prized photo albums. There was always a Werther's or dessert mint to enjoy nearby. Being with her was a treat. Sharing her stories and pictures of her friends and family made her beam with pride. They were everything to her.

Seeing my dad take care of her throughout the years made my heart grow for both of them. I feel honored to have witnessed their mutual respect and love for each other.

No one is perfect, although I felt she loved me perfectly. With her whole heart and soul. With every ounce of her being. I hope I can love others the way she loved me.

My hope is that we practice the many lessons she taught us. May we see the goodness in others as she did. May we find joy in the simple pleasures of life. A shared conversation with a loved one, watching birds, appreciating nature and each other. May we live our lives in a way that honors her.

Rest in peace, Grandma Margaret. You are forever and ever loved.

When I finished, I took my seat, fighting back tears—tears of sadness because I had lost this special person and tears of gratitude because I was able to find the words to describe our relationship and share what she meant to me.

Note-writing transformed me so profoundly that I was able to speak about my grandmother from a place of light and truth. What will it enable you to do?

Metamorphosis

When I think of transformation, I can't help but think of butterflies. The transformation of a caterpillar into a butterfly is one of the most remarkable examples of metamorphosis in the natural world. The process involves a complete restructuring of the caterpillar's body, as it transforms from a chunky, crawling, leaf-eating bug into a delicate, beautiful, flying creature with wings.

In many ways, the caterpillar's journey reflects our human experience. There is nothing wrong with being exactly who you are right now, even if you are a chunky green bug. However, just as the caterpillar undergoes a transformation to reach its full potential, we too must embrace change and growth to flourish as individuals. Change is a part of life.

The act of restructuring yourself offers a chance to embrace a new way of being. Necessary change doesn't always feel good but results in a new, more vibrant being. Keep in mind you are not transforming for anyone else; after all, a caterpillar has nothing to prove to anyone. You are shedding your old skin because it is the natural way of things.

In the rest of this chapter, I offer up some of the ways I feel I was transformed over my year of note-writing; I predict the practice can work similarly for you.

Channeling Energy

I've struggled with self-discipline since I was young, particularly when it comes to sweets. When my dad—a fellow cookie lover—turned forty, he had lots of cookies at his party. When I say *lots*, I mean *lots*, and they were the good kind: Cookies by Design. While the adults overindulged in alcohol, I overindulged in sugar cookies. Approximately ten to fifteen, according to memory. "How do you keep down this many sugar cookies?" you ask. You don't. I ended up feeling sick and throwing up. My parents were not pleased.

Austin, who is a disciplined person, sometimes remarks on this tendency of mine to be undisciplined. Although I don't like being labeled this way, I recognize that there is some truth to it. This realization, along with a desire to become more disciplined, led me to take this note-writing challenge personally. Writing a note every day wasn't exactly the same kind of discipline as not eating fifteen cookies at a party, but it was discipline, nonetheless. I was determined to follow through with this commitment.

Not only was this challenge a way to improve my discipline, but also it helped me grow my self-worth, confidence, and belief in myself. Every day, I proved to myself that I was capable of setting and achieving goals no matter how strange or lofty. I kept this promise to myself over and over again. This newfound discipline lit me up on the inside. I felt proud of myself and I learned that I could achieve anything I set my mind to. I stuck to the course, writing while persevering through a year full of challenges when I was living in multiple cities. I could do anything I set my mind on doing. Through this focused energy, I was able to find a world that had been hiding from me in plain sight. I became more open and receptive to my experience and the world around me.

We can choose where we focus our attention in our limited time. And we should, because it matters. As Qui-Gon said in *Star Wars*, "Your focus determines your reality." By focusing my attention on a daily practice of writing notes, my relationship with myself improved, and I started showing up differently in the world. My consistency gave me purpose and fulfillment. Note by note, I transformed into a more disciplined and confident version of myself.

I still eat the cookies, but not all at once; now, I savor each one.

Increased Vibrancy

Writing handwritten notes was also a personal way for me to combat laziness. I'm talking about transforming my lethargy into energy. How is this possible? It's because note-writing is an energy giver: an avenue to raising your vibration, providing feelings of newfound purpose and passion.

Devoting attention to others through handwritten notes will fill you with vibrancy, inspiration, and the spirit of life. Why? Because you'll connect with your spirit and see the spirit in others.

I get jazzed about handwritten notes. I thoroughly enjoy every step of the process: imagining them, writing them, sending them, and reading them again once the receivers receive them. I even read my sent notes again when I need a little extra oomph—another reason for keeping copies. In every step, I find true, genuine enjoyment. Not surface-level dopamine hits like when you get a like on Instagram, but genuine joy. Writing notes has raised my vibrancy. It makes me feel good. If feeling jazzed is the goal, and it should be, then handwritten notes are the way.

Decreased Fear/Increased Interest

The notes helped me shift my mindset from the fear of uncontrollable, nonstop change and uncertainty into curiosity. They helped me realize that the unknown was not a place to be scared of—it was a place to explore and expand into. It turned out the world was a place of opportunity, newness, and growth. It was full of possibilities.

There is so much going on out there that we are not aware of—people, places, animals, and things. We can't take it all in; we are limited by our senses, and even if we weren't, the sheer volume of information is overwhelming. It's like we are only aware of experiencing one single grain of sand on an entire beach in a world full of beaches. Writing notes forced me to tap into these small yet significant details. I would highlight them to make the notes special and to connect with the recipient in the best way I knew how.

Even with people we think we "know" well, we only know a snippet of their world. By showing interest—by really listening to others and what they have to say, by exploring the depths of their being—we can move out of fear. By focusing on interest, exploration, and curiosity, we can move our focus away from ourselves. We redirect our attention toward learning and gathering information. The more we explore our genuine interest in others and the world around us, the more beauty we will see and the more magic we will discover. Instead of getting stuck in fear, we can invest ourselves in taking a deeper interest in the world around us.

The notes were a way to dig deeper into my life experience, to train my mind to find the good and express what was going right. To catch glimpses of the special. To tap into the magic of a kind word or a small act that I might have missed before. This is where the magic lives.

Increased Passion

I was always envious of people who knew exactly what they wanted to do in life. With a specific passion to pursue—per Merriam-Webster, passion is an "intense, driving, or overmastering feeling or conviction"—they could follow a set path. My path, in contrast, seemed foggy and unclear. I'm sure that's why I waited until I was forced by my college to declare a major at the end of my sophomore year.

Of course, I changed my major again senior year, though I was homing in on a direction with general human ecology. Human ecology is an interdisciplinary and transdisciplinary study of the relationship between humans and their natural, social, and built environments. In other words, it is the applied human science that studies the question of everyday life, with a goal of helping others.

You are probably wondering what you do with a general human ecology degree, and so were my parents. When my family asked me this very question, I eagerly, if not very helpfully, replied, "I can do anything!" We still laugh about my response. I smile at this past version of me because I am still her in many ways. I still dream big dreams and pursue out-of-the-ordinary experiences.

Today, though, I've learned to harness my passions. I've found a nontraditional way to practice helping others while learning more about humans along the way.

Increased Acceptance

Part of personal growth is accepting what was not meant for you and letting it go with grace. Writing notes can help you move through this process by learning from each encounter and recognizing that every relationship teaches valuable lessons. This is a more helpful way to move forward than denying the past. Believe me, I've tried pretending certain events never happened and certain people never existed. Ignoring parts of myself and parts of my life I wasn't proud of only created a confusing sense of separation within me.

I am no longer going to ignore these parts of myself. They are a part of me and my evolution, and I am ready to face them head-on. In that spirit, I wrote a note to my ex to thank him. This seemed wild and unusual because we hadn't been in contact for multiple years.

A note to an ex:

> *Thank you for teaching me that I need to love myself first. To stop looking for external validation. To stop depending on you and on other people for my happiness. To look inside myself instead. Thank you for the pain; it led me on a journey of self-discovery. It took time, although I found my light again. I started to shine. I learned how to respect myself and to demand respect from anyone I let into my life. I learned how to set boundaries to protect myself. To protect my heart. The heart I was so eager to give away in the hope of receiving love in return. The years of tears and shame were messy and dark, but they were mine, and they make the joy taste even sweeter. Thank you for these lessons. I wouldn't be the woman I am today without them.*
>
> *I hope you can find joy too.*
>
> *Kristen*

Reflecting on the lessons learned during and after our relationship allowed me to maintain forward motion on my life path with appreciation, understanding, and well-wishes. To keep growing and keep going. I listened to my intuition and took note! (See what I did there?)

I admit, letting go is easier said than done. Same with moving forward. Sometimes I get stuck and stagnant from gripping onto what I think I need to survive. Writing notes is an exercise to help you move through, move forward, and move on. These notes might bring up some things you didn't realize you were still holding on to. Breathe. Continue writing. Stick to the program, not for the recipient, but for you.

You don't have to stay stuck. You can move forward, get better, expand your existence. You can find inner freedom. You can improve with time. By creating a habit of writing handwritten notes, you are investing in yourself. Change will happen, and the sky is the limit.

Increased Self-Understanding

I often surprised myself with the thoughts and feelings that came out as I wrote. This creative contemplation helped me to uncover deep emotions, and with practice, I became better at understanding these feelings and connecting the dots of my thoughts. Additionally, I discovered an abundance of appreciation. I found myself feeling grateful to the many people, places, and experiences that enriched my life. A single note per day could hardly capture the magnitude of gratitude I held within me.

Instead of walking unconsciously through life, as I did during much of my twenties, I started appreciating and actually paying attention to the world around me. These days, I pause to stop and smell the flowers during walks with my dog, leaving my phone behind. I reach out and touch the trees, appreciating a moment under their shade, marveling at their age. I've developed a deep love and admiration for the natural world. Notes have reoriented my focus on life, inspiring me to become an active participant in what is happening instead of just being along for the ride as a passive bystander. I feel intimately connected and closer to myself, my soul, my intuition, and the person I was always meant to be.

There is a saying that at the end of your life, hell is when you meet the person you could have been—a haunting reminder of missed opportunities. In this vision, I imagine that idealized version of me is a person who writes a fuck-ton of notes. And so I choose to embody and be her now because I really don't want her to haunt me later.

As I wrote, I also came to realize there were parts of me still waiting to be discovered. I was leaning into this creative, fun person, making room for her to express herself, to create and do her own thing, to shine. And I was enjoying my time with her. She was silly yet thoughtful. She was quirky and spunky, whimsical and fun. She embodied the person I aspired to be, so I offered her the creative space to explore, play, laugh, cry, and appreciate. She was the part of me I wanted to grow.

What an unexpected and delightful surprise it was to find there was more to discover about myself. That there was this creator in me I didn't recognize before. Writing handwritten notes helped me find missing pieces of myself. I'm finally feeling like I'm stepping into my own shoes, ready to walk—or skip—forward, full of enthusiasm and purpose.

I also learned to appreciate things about myself that I'd previously seen as flaws. Growing up, I was often labeled as "sensitive" by those around me. I felt things deeply and would cry easily, which was not viewed as a strength. In fact, I was often told not to cry, which confused me. I realize now I was being told to suppress my emotions, which made me feel ashamed. Why was I not allowed to feel? Were feelings bad? Or were just the "bad" feelings bad? I felt like a problem and my feelings felt like a disability. I began to view my sensitivity as a weakness that I needed to try to overcome. It was exhausting.

However, I eventually realized that my sensitivity was not a flaw but rather a gift. Through the art of note-writing, I discovered that I could channel my emotions and intuition into something meaningful. I realized that sensitivity is a positive trait. A superpower. I could use my sensitivity to feel more deeply into relationships and words. I could reflect and share. I could use my sensitivity as a gift—as an asset instead of a liability.

Increased Positivity

Through this journey, I was connected to another person who practiced note-writing. Birds of a feather fly together! We met over coffee and shared our experiences. We agreed it was challenging to put into words the benefits we received from this practice. We agreed upon self-growth, increased connection to ourselves, more confidence, greater ability to express ourselves, positive happenings, relationship transformation with others, and the increase of heart-warmth. We were both brought to tears by our note-writing practices. Our lives have been positively changed by the amount of shared meaning we discovered.

Hearing this gal share some of the same benefits I also experienced was invigorating. It made me even more sure of my mission to revive the art of creating handwritten notes. I knew it was possible for other people to experience some—if not all—of the same transformative benefits.

When I think back on my own personal transformation, I think I was meant to write these notes so I could speak at my grandma's funeral with an open heart. I was meant to practice capturing the essence of people for a year, feeling into their shared humanity and capturing their light with words. It was the practice I needed to honor her in the best way I could. This practice can transform you, too, in unimaginable ways, preparing you to be your best for what's to come.

More positive things will come your way when you acknowledge the good in others. Positivity will naturally flow into your life experience. You will look for the positive in others and everything around you. In turn, you will hold positive expectations, and your life experience will transform in a beautiful way. The universe will seem to work in your favor, on the same team. Coincidences, synchronicities, signs, and opportunities will appear. The positivity you emit will be reflected back to you exponentially.

I know it seems like a lot, but I do believe that this simple act of self-expression will set you on a path of endless possibilities, transforming the way you see and exist in the world. I predict it will unleash your authentic voice, increase your vitality, catalyze your growth, enhance your sense of fulfillment, deepen your empathy, align your actions with who you really are, amplify your positivity, and unleash your creativity.

As you evolve and grow, you will begin to show up in life with a greater sense of authenticity, gratitude, and self-awareness, inspiring you to be the best version of yourself. Over time, you will train yourself to look for the magic and meaning in every moment, unlocking your inner potential and creating the life of your dreams. This journey will leave you feeling more open, receptive, and connected to the world around you, fueling your personal evolution and creating a lasting impact on your inner and outer worlds.

Are you ready to light up yourself and your relationships? In Part II, I'll show you how. Let's jump in.

Part II:

Developing a Note-Writing Practice, Step by Step

In this section, we will dive deeper into mindful preparation for writing notes by setting conscious intentions and goals to help us make the most of this practice. We will also explore the different occasions for writing notes and the limitless possibilities of who we can write them to. So, let's tap into our creativity and imagination as we embark on this journey of creating meaningful notes.

Chapter Eight:

Mindful Preparation

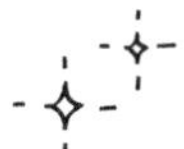

At this point, you may be thinking you'd like to start writing handwritten notes, but you don't know where to begin. You may already be wondering who to write to and what to say. Those are important choices, but first, let's prepare ourselves by getting into the right mindset. I find that to really enter the moment when you write these notes, it can help to do some simple mindfulness exercises. Meditating puts me in a better headspace to relax and express myself. I like to make the process of creating notes as enjoyable as possible, because why not?

Put yourself in a place where you feel comfortable, eliminate or limit distractions, and allow yourself to drop into the zone. If you can ease your way into a flow state, you are making big moves. A nice way to set yourself up for success is to start with a ten-minute meditation.

Meditation is a helpful tool to clear your mind and center your heart. Meditation can also help improve your focus and attention. Please feel welcome to lengthen or shorten this time. If you are new to meditation or prefer guided meditation, I recommend the Happier or Gaia apps. After you meditate, put yourself in the best space you can to drop into heart opening.

Elevate Your Senses

Elevate your senses to optimize your note-writing experience and make this practice delightful. Because, again, why not? By engaging different senses, you can stimulate your creativity and enhance the overall experience, making it more enjoyable and satisfying. The more you expose yourself to different sensory experiences, the more sensitive you will become. Test some or all of these sensory activity ideas to stimulate your creativity and craft an ideal note-writing experience for yourself.

Touch

The tactile sensation of the pen and the physical qualities of the paper are important aspects of touch. Are you using pens and paper that feel good to work with? Do you have a favorite pen? One that feels nice to hold and writes just right? Your pen and paper preferences will emerge through trial and error. The more you explore, the better you will understand your likes and dislikes.

Similarly, where are you seated? Have you found a comfortable and relaxed position? Do you prefer to work indoors or outdoors? Take the time to experiment with different seating options to find a spot where you can feel at ease. Try sitting on different types of seats with a variety of materials to experience a range of textures. Consider sitting at a desk or on a picnic blanket outside to further explore your preferences. Personally, I find sitting on a soft, furry blanket enjoyable. The beauty is that you can take your notes with you, so you can do this anywhere you can bring a pen and paper.

Sight

What does your ideal note-writing space look like? Imagine the perfect environment. What would you like to see in the background? Is it a cozy corner? Your favorite chair? A local coffee shop? A library? Consider lighting. What suits your mood and preferences? Do you feel more comfortable indoors or is natural sunlight calling you?

Narrow in on the location that sparks your creativity. For example, you might choose a place that holds special meaning to you and the recipient, maybe a place you enjoyed together; as you look around, you'll be filled with the spirit of shared memories that can spark your writing.

Sound

Sound can be a powerful tool to enhance the note-writing process. Explore the ability of music to set the tone for your creative flow. Music and creativity go together—listening to music can significantly enhance the flow of ideas. What type of music helps your creative juices flow?

For my note-writing practice, I've curated two "Inspiration" playlists on Spotify. Both contain a variety of low-key songs that heighten my emotions, elevate my mood, and inspire heartfelt expression. One of the playlists is "sans words" because sometimes lyrics distract me. I also enjoy classical piano compositions, especially by Beethoven and Hans Zimmer, who integrates electronic music with traditional orchestra.

When writing to someone you know well, you might immerse yourself in their favorite songs, artists, or genres to better understand and connect with them. To trigger memories, you could listen to sounds you both love—ocean waves or birds chirping in the morning.

Then again, you might be called to create in silence. Consider your preferences, as words or music in general may be disruptive. Find what works best for you—choose your own adventure to find the right balance of inspiration and focus to expand your creative horizons.

Taste

Why not indulge in your favorite beverage while writing, whether it's coffee, a smoothie, tea, or sparkling water? If I'm writing in the morning, it's a cold brew. If I'm writing in the afternoon, I prefer a Topo Chico. Whatever it is, find a way to make it a special experience, even if it's just water—pour it into a fun cup or your favorite mug.

Treat yourself to something enjoyable during or after your writing session as well. A little positive reinforcement never hurt anyone. It can be a great motivator. I prefer Lily's dark chocolate peanut butter cups.

Smell

Engage your sniffer to enhance your writing process. Choose scents that uplift, inspire, or are just downright enjoyable. It could be the aroma of coffee beans in your local coffee shop, the fresh air on your porch or in your favorite spot at the park, the fragrance of your favorite scented candle or incense, or even the scent of freshly picked flowers from your garden. If you find comfort in the presence of your furry friend, a quick sniff of their familiar fur can provide a sense of warmth and connection while you write.

By optimizing your senses, you create an immersive and enriching note-writing experience. Enjoy the process as you embark on a journey of creativity and self-expression.

Cultivate a Giving Mindset

The mindset with which we write and send a note matters. As Sharon Salzberg says in her book *Real Love*, "It's most loving if our offerings are made freely, without strings attached." This powerful sentiment resonated deeply with me after a personal experience.

I had hosted a baby shower for my friend, as well as a wedding shower and a bachelorette party before that. I put a lot of effort and money into planning these events to make them special. However, I never received a thank-you note from my friend (though many, many months later, she did thank me by taking us out to get massages). As a "words of affirmation" gal, this left me feeling disappointed and unappreciated. I found it difficult to let go of this perceived oversight. I realized I had some lingering resentment toward my friend, and my negative emotions had started to affect our friendship.

At first, this experience motivated me to write more notes to the people in my life, so *they* wouldn't feel unappreciated or unacknowledged. I wanted to express how much they meant to me and make sure they knew it.

However, as I continued along this note-writing journey, I realized that I had been approaching this with the wrong mindset all along. I needed to check myself. Examine my own perspective. A note is not an obligation or an expectation—a note is a gift. Just like any gift, it represents your love, time, effort, creativity, and expression. And just like any gift, a note should be given freely, without expecting anything in return or even an acknowledgment of receiving it.

I repeat: Do not expect to receive anything in return. We must give our gifts from a place of pure love—a love that asks for nothing back. They are offerings from the heart, with no strings attached.

This experience served as a profound reminder for me to examine my mindset, intentions, and the state of my heart when giving. I learned to offer my love and gratitude simply and freely. As I continue on this journey, I remind myself to begin each note in this state of mind.

Mindfulness will prepare you to move from a place of love, as well. Having taken the time to mentally and physically prepare yourself to write, you are now equipped to give your words freely and joyfully, without any expectations. Through this process you have also discovered ways to infuse joy into your unique approach to writing notes. Now you are ready to take the next step.

Chapter Nine:

The Power of Words

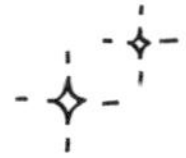

Sawubona: "I see you."

How many times a day do you have an exchange like this?

"Hi, how are you?"

"Good, good."

We say these words so much, they become automatic and, too often, inauthentic.

While researching the depth of greetings in other languages, I discovered that in Zulu culture, there is a greeting that holds deep meaning called *Sawubona*. Translated as "I see you," Sawubona invites us to truly witness and be present with others. Saying it shows that we recognize and respect each person's unique journey in life. This greeting made a strong impression on me, reminding me of the importance of treating others with respect and truly seeing them for who they are. The heartfelt witnessing inherent in the Zulu language inspired me.

This Zulu greeting sets a remarkable standard for writing notes. It teaches us to acknowledge others, truly see them, understand their perspective (to the best of our ability), and embrace our shared humanity. It encourages us to give the precious gifts of recognition and love. Hello, note-writing goals!

Being seen matters. We all long to be truly seen, to be understood, and to share our souls beyond the masks we wear for the world, our jobs, or our families. For instance, I was recently introduced to a life coach by a friend, and instead of simply listing my job title or where I was from in the introductory email, my friend described me as "Devotion, Wonder, Sanctuary, Wisdom, and Peace." What a difference that made. Those powerful words made me feel seen and understood in a way that a job title or label never could. Those words shined a light on positive attributes that I would not have recognized in myself before.

Words can do more than help us appreciate—words can manifest. Our words are like magic spells, and we are constantly casting them into the universe. Words have power. And with this power comes great responsibility. We can use our words to warm a lonely soul, comfort a broken heart, or bring a smile to a face. We can use our words to spread positivity, build and mend relationships, help others see the good in themselves, and create joy.

Alternatively, we can use our words to hurt, divide, and spread negativity. Therefore, it's important to choose our words carefully and intentionally. Let us use our words to cast spells of wonder, delight, and positivity. Let us use our words to speak our truth and forge deep, meaningful connections with others. Let us use our words to dream big and encourage others to do the same.

Imagine if we acknowledged others in this way, by pinpointing the goodness we see in them, rather than assigning superficial labels. It would be a powerful and meaningful way to connect with one another and create a world filled with positivity and love. Remember, the universe is listening, and our words may outlive us. Each word we choose can take us one step closer to the world we want to live in. Let us use them to create a world we are proud to leave behind.

Establishing Intention

To begin, let's establish clear intentions by aiming to infuse our notes with love and sincerity.

Through our notes, we aspire to uplift, to serve, and to empower. Each word is an opportunity to acknowledge the inherent value of the recipient, affirming their worth and significance in our lives. As we write, we strive to uncover the truth as we understand it in our hearts and transfer it onto paper, making the intangible tangible.

Our primary goal is to thoughtfully consider the recipient while honoring our own voice. We aim to write honestly and authentically, guided by our heart's truth. With vulnerability and openness, we strive to convey how we experience others, diving deep into our emotions and transmuting them into carefully chosen phrases and words.

By manifesting our thoughts and emotions into the physical world, we give life to our intentions. We bring them to life on the page. The act of writing becomes a conduit through which we can connect and communicate in a profound way. May our notes be infused with love, authenticity, and purpose as we embark on this transformative journey of sharing our innermost selves with others.

Notes for Every Occasion

I realize these are some lofty goals. I share them to inspire you, not to scare you, though.

Notes don't always have to be serious. They don't always have to be anything. In the words of Elizabeth Gilbert, author of *Big Magic*, "... say what you want to say ... and say it with all your heart. Share whatever you are driven to share."

You don't need a special occasion to write a note either. You can write a note for any occasion or for no occasion at all.

Let's explore the various occasions that could inspire you to pick up your pen. We have the ready-made classics: graduations, weddings, anniversaries, engagements, promotions, and accomplishments. You can find countless traditional holidays on the calendar. And people are always celebrating something new—babies, houses, jobs, even the companionship of new furry friends.

But, hey, why limit yourself? You can also write a note just because. You can celebrate the fun times with a note for a bachelor or bachelorette party. Pen words of support and encouragement to those battling illness or going through recovery. You can craft a message to lift someone's spirits or express gratitude to someone who brightened your day.

Let's not overlook moments of loss, whether it's the passing of a beloved pet or a dear human. Birthdays, thank-you notes, sobriety achievement dates, apologies, hosting events ... and the list goes on: all opportunities to express your caring.

Don't feel constrained by specific occasions. You have the power to create your own occasion. Your note is an extension of you: a gift, an intentional act of service, an expression of love. It's your hand, reaching out to connect with others. So listen closely to that little bird on your shoulder, whispering ideas into your ear. You could write to that person, or you could even write to the little bird itself. Let the ideas swirl, be open to your inspiration, and welcome your creativity. There are notes within you. All we need to do is draw them out onto paper and into the world.

Who (and What) to Write To

So far, we've explored the countless reasons for picking up the pen, and we've seen how our words can hold great power. The thing is, the power of words increases exponentially when the words are given to another. There has to be someone—or something—on the other end of your communication. So it's important to choose who to write to with the same mindfulness we've brought to our other preparations.

Let your imagination soar. Embrace the freedom and opportunity that lie before you. There is no limit to the number of notes you can write or the reasons behind them. No one is stopping you! The ideas are churning. The inspiration is building. We are feeling wild with freedom, inspiration, and the opportunity to connect with any person, place, or thing we want to. Opportunities await!

Writing to . . . Other Humans

At the risk of stating the obvious, there are humans who need your notes. Which ones, you may ask? That's up to you to decide! Let's dive in, we can't keep them waiting!

Let's start by generating ideas about who you would like to write to. You can consider people of your past, present, or future. You might choose a mentor, family member, or friend. You could write to someone you've met, an acquaintance, or even a stranger.

I invite you to tune into the receiver, to drop into the essence of the person you are writing to. Envision them in your mind. How do they look? Are they smiling? How do they make you feel? What is coming through? Tap into that essence so you can write with an open heart. Be as truthful as possible. Don't be afraid to get vulnerable.

This requires receptivity, engaging with your whole body, and making an effort to truly understand and connect with the other person. Imagine you are turning on your radio receiver and adjusting the dial to find the note receiver's radio station. Tuning into their frequency. Tapping into their reality. By actively listening in, you demonstrate genuine interest and create a space for deeper communication and understanding.

Meditator Matthew Hepburn breaks a gratitude meditation down into three steps in his guided meditations on the Happier app. I invite you to try these steps when writing a note, as well:

1. Remembering the good
2. Heightening the memory
3. Expressing sincere thanks (also saying it out loud)

It's easy to get jazzed about the possibility of writing a handwritten note to someone you love. Feel the thrill of the thought of writing to someone you look up to or admire—your favorite musician, artist, author, poet, or creator. You never know who might write you back until you try! I wrote to one of my favorite authors, Adam Grant, who wrote *Think Again*, and he wrote me an email back.

But why stop there? Get jazzed about writing to your accountant, your dermatologist, your therapist, or even the president! The possibilities are limitless, my friend. This is the ultimate freedom of expression, and nobody can stop you! If you're not sure who to write to first, you can get started with family, friends, neighbors, doctors, dentists, teachers, mentors, government officials, bosses, and coworkers.

The list really is endless. For example, here is a list of some of the human beings I wrote notes to:

friends near and far, a friend's mom, a newborn baby, my beloved family members, neighbors, dogsitters, my high school mythology teacher, colleagues, acquaintances, the owner of an adorable Italian greyhound, an AT&T service provider, my plumber, a Facebook Marketplace couch seller, an AirBnb host, restaurant servers, small-business owners, a holiday train set attendant at the mall, landscapers and groundskeepers, my eyebrow waxer, a meditation coach, doctors and therapists, dental hygienists, caregivers, healers, community leaders, musicians, the co-director of *My Octopus Teacher*, authors, a dog-portrait artist

You can write a note to anyone! Literally any human. We were at the grocery store over the holidays, and I dropped a can of queso, and it exploded everywhere. I was embarrassed. The cashier was so kind and made me feel better. She was busy, working the holidays, and still made room for kindness and love.

A note to a grocery cashier:

Thank you for working over the holidays on Christmas Eve's eve to help us get stocked up on food. I appreciate your kindness and positive attitude. You made me feel comfortable even after I dropped the can of queso. Your understanding made my embarrassment more bearable. Thank you.

With gratitude and love,
Kristen

Your note could provide that ounce of encouragement someone desperately needs. It could make them feel noticed and validated, reminding them that their efforts are worthwhile. As @veekster on X wisely posted, "If you are moved by someone, by someone's work, by their friendship, anything—TELL THEM. You don't know how much they might need that ounce of encouragement, to feel noticed, to feel like their efforts are worthwhile."[21]

A SPECIAL CASE: SYMPATHY NOTES

Acknowledging your reason for writing is, of course, easiest when you are offering thanks or praise. Yet some of the most important notes express or acknowledge sorrow. Sometimes, life isn't so sunny. Loss is a part of life. While we cannot take away another person's pain, we can offer comfort through our words.

At the same time, we must recognize that grief is a deeply personal and complex emotion, and what brings solace to one person may not resonate with another. And even as we feel called to find words that acknowledge their pain and convey genuine empathy, we may fear saying the wrong thing and unintentionally causing more pain.

Personally, I find these words the most challenging to express. They often get stuck within me. The "stuckness" comes from a good place—a genuine desire to provide support and solace during difficult times. This desire exists because we understand, to some degree at least, the pain they are feeling. And at the same time, it's challenging to confront and accept our own feelings of loss, sadness, and grief, paradoxically making it harder to find the "right" words to offer comfort, empathy, support, and love to others.

---

21. Victoria Wright (@veekster), "If you are moved by someone, by someone's work, by their friendship, anything—TELL THEM. Twitter (now X), May 19, 2021, https://twitter.com/veekster/status/1395080305761918976?lang=en.

Along my journey, I've gathered examples and phrases that may assist you in crafting your own sympathy notes. Use whichever words feel genuine and resonate with you. For example:

Today is a hard day. It's the kind I want to protect you from. The kind I want to fix and make better so you don't have to feel the pain. I know that is impossible. Instead, I will be here to hold space for you. For your sadness. I'm here to remind you that you aren't alone. My heart is with you every day. Especially today. Sending the biggest hug.

May you be free from your pain. May you be free of your sorrow. May you be free of suffering. May you feel comfort. May you feel surrounded by love. May you be at ease. May your suffering be eased. May your heart be at peace. I care about you. I care about your suffering. You are in my thoughts. You have been on my mind. You are in my prayers. Sending you big wishes and prayers for healing. May you feel enveloped by the love of your family and friends. Get well soon.

Get Specific

By actively listening, you also tune into the specific details that will be meaningful to the recipient of your note. Being specific in your note-writing adds depth and thoughtfulness and leaves a lasting impression on the recipient. By including meaningful details about the person or your shared experiences, you show that you are genuinely attentive and interested. Let's take a closer look at an example.

A note to my nail tech:

Thank you for my awesome chrome nails! They look so cool and got me jazzed up for my trip. What a treat. I enjoyed talking with you about Haiti and Miami. Wishing you a great rest of the year and best of luck finishing up with your degrees in sociology/chemistry.

With gratitude and love,
Kristen

In this note, I made a point to recall specific details from our conversation, demonstrating my genuine interest in the recipient's experience. By mentioning the pursuit of her degrees and referring to our discussion, I showed attentiveness to her aspirations.

If the recipient spoke to you about something specific that resonated with you, tell them. If a certain characteristic shined through them, let them know. This level of specificity conveys sincerity and connection.

Don't just trust your brain to remember the details, though. Take notes! After that conversation with my nail tech about her finishing school, I made a quick note on my phone so I could remember the degrees she was working on. If someone mentions something specific, such as their plans, interests, experiences, an upcoming vacation, an event, or their studies, write it down. This allows you to incorporate those details into your note and wish them well.

More pointers for getting specific:

- Recall specific details. Refer back to specific conversations, experiences, or aspects of the person's life that stood out to you. This demonstrates your attentiveness and shows that you value and remember the things they share with you.
- Acknowledge the recipient's uniqueness, their special gifts, and what they bring to the table.

> When you are tuned into their unique essence, you can recognize their spirit. Speak directly to that by mentioning specific characteristics, talents, or strengths that you appreciate about them.

Speak from the heart. When being specific, be genuine and heartfelt in your words. Sharing your truth and vulnerability helps create a deeper connection. The more of each you can share, the better. You will feel the truth when it comes out. Your recipient will feel it too.

Writing to . . . Nonhumans

Your note recipient doesn't have to be a human. Humans are not the only creatures to call Earth home! It's time to open our minds and get creative!

I spoke earlier of writing to the little bird on your shoulder, and I meant it. Handwritten notes can help you connect with animals, nature, times, places, and walks of life that are different from your own.

For example, during my note-writing journey, I wrote a note to the place I temporarily called home: Florida. Writing to a place helped me forge a deeper connection with my environment and appreciate its unique offerings, such as the diverse wildlife, weather, and scenery. I encourage you to try writing to a place, animal, or thing that has been important in your life, noticing its gifts, creatures, feels, weather, sounds, smells, and vibes.

A note to a place, named "An Ode to Florida":

> *Thank you, Florida creatures—my new friends. Wood storks welcoming the morning sun, big bodies and leathery heads gathered high in the trees. Two roosters freely roaming the neighborhood with a true sense of belonging.*

Baby snakes slithering across the road. Palm trees standing proudly, supplying berries, a tasty fruit to many birds. Ospreys swirling and nose-diving in the hopes of catching a fish for lunch. Anhingas swimming. Popping their snake-like heads above the water in the shape of a hook. My favorite bird, a delightful sight. Cranes weathering Hurricane Elsa, huddled together with unwavering strength. An inspiration. Intricate webs above the driveway, brought to you by our local artist, the orb-weaving spider. Frog symphonies in the pond, loud and proud through the night. The stars shining brightly over the dark ocean, reminding me of my size in the vast universe. I am grateful for days on the back patio in my bikini. Red dots up and down my body. A gift from the no-see-ums. A price I am willing to pay to bear witness to the wildlife and its magic. The beauty is life-giving and breathtaking at the same time. Feeling a part of it is the gift.

A note to Earth (on Earth Day):

Thank you for being my home. For giving, housing, feeding, and nurturing. I am in awe of your magnificence. Especially your furry creatures, sunsets, and ocean waves. I get lost in the beauty of your trees and mountains. I feel connected through your animals, especially hummingbirds, butterflies, and dogs. I feel at home outdoors. Feet in the dirt, grass, or sand in between my toes. Sometimes I lose my way, but I am my best when I feel our bond. I feel a part of you. Inextricably linked together as one. I am a blip on your timeline, but you mean the world to me. I promise to use my water bottle whenever possible, to pick up loose trash, to recycle, and to treat you with the TLC you deserve.

With respect, love, and admiration, your earthling,

Kristen

A note to trees, named "An Ode to Trees":

I salute your strong trunks
Your reaching arms
Your leaves that go with the flow
Giving, but not throwing, shade
Standing tall and proud
With your mesmerizing shades of green
You are me and I am you and
We are one

And what about animals? I know what you're thinking—my dog doesn't know how to read! It doesn't matter. Even though they may not be able to read what we write, writing a heartfelt note to our furry (or scaly, or bald—no discrimination here) friends can be a powerful way to express our love and appreciation for them.

I wrote a note to my dog, thanking him for bringing joy and companionship into my life. He has been my source of comfort and support, and our adventures together have created cherished memories. In my note, I celebrated his unique personality and the transformative effect he had on my perceptions. Dogs, and animals in general, teach us valuable lessons about love, joy, and living authentically. Sharing these heartfelt words with our animal companions can create beautiful moments of connection and understanding.

A note to my dog, Sosa:

Little butter dog, thank you for bringing so much joy to my life. I love the way you are. Being in your presence brings me peace and calm. Unofficially, you are my emotional support dog. You've helped me through my darkest days. You've also been there for the best of days. Being with you makes it the best. Our RV trip through Yellowstone was so special. I loved exploring the great outdoors with you! It made me smile seeing you excited about all the new smells! Before you were mine, I believed the stereotypes about pit bulls. Can you believe it?! My biggest concern was that you might "turn on me." I love telling this story because it is unbelievably funny to anyone who knows you. You are the sweetest, dopiest guy. I love the way you show affection and give lots of licks. You transformed my views and prejudices by just being yourself. The moment I saw your little piggie face, I knew we were meant to be. I asked which dog was the nicest. The lady said, "the meek one" and pointed to the sweet pup at her feet. You were special. You always will be. They say humans are not worthy of dogs, and I agree. We have so much to learn from you. Although your life is shorter, I've heard it's because you already know the right way to live. You love truly, fully, and unconditionally. You spread pure joy. What more could I ask for? Thank you for being the light of my life. I love you the way you love beef, and that's a lot.

Love and licks,
Your proud mom (and Instagram manager)

Go ahead. Write your animals a note. Write your friend's animals a note. I read my dog's note to him out loud. It was such a special moment; I was moved to tears.

Or, if you aren't an animal person, maybe you're a plant person. Try writing to your plant, or any plant inside or outside. Research shows plants grow more if you talk to them. If this is true, and I believe it is, imagine what happens to humans when you speak nicely to them, when they read your words through a handwritten note. We are growing plants, animals, and humans! We are helping living beings reach their greatest potential with handwritten notes! Because science! We can do anything when the universe is on our side . . . and it is!

Writing nonhuman notes connected me back to nature and the feeling of oneness. As Carl Jung so beautifully put it, "At times I feel as if I am spread out over the landscape and inside things and am myself living in every tree, in the splashing of the waves, in the clouds and animals that come and go, in the procession of the seasons."[22]

Writing nonhuman notes challenged me to widen my reach, to extend my gratitude further. To notice and appreciate more than my fellow humans. My nonhuman notes challenged me to look around, feel into the landscape, my plant neighbors, the sky, the Earth. As my appreciation flowed to new places, I dared to color outside of the lines, creating something more than an ordinary thank-you note.

Inspiration might come from the tree that provides a refuge of shade, the blooming flower that brightens your walk, the squirrel's funny game of chase around the tree that makes you giggle, or an outdoor stroll during your favorite season. It might come from catching a bird's eye while you enjoy their song, sharing a moment and knowing you are more alike than different. Note-writing helped me notice how interconnected everything really is. Like Jung said, "It is not only possible but fairly probable, even, that psyche and matter are two different aspects of one and the same thing."[23]

So write a note to the Grand Canyon, write a note to the pet snake you follow on Instagram, write a note to a place that touched your soul. Challenge yourself, use your imagination, write a note, and see where it takes you.

---

22. Carl Jung, *Memories, Dreams, Reflections* (Vintage Books, 1989), 225.

23. Carl Jung, *Synchronicity: An Acasual Connecting Principle* (Princeton University Press, 2010).

Writing to . . . Yourself

But wait, you might be thinking, *what about me? Can I write a note to myself?* Why yes, I'd recommend that you do!

At a recent note-writing workshop, I surprised everyone by asking them to begin by writing a note of gratitude to themselves instead of someone else. Many participants, including my mother at age sixty-two, had never written a note of gratitude to themselves before. How quick we are to forget about ourselves. To extend love to others without first filling our cup. But we can't pour from an empty cup. The relationship we have with ourselves is the foundation of every other relationship we have.

That's why I invite you to go ahead, write a note to yourself. It can be your current self, past self, inner child, future self, whichever *you* you feel inclined to speak to. You deserve your time, love, compassion, and self-gratitude.

For example, you might practice self-gratitude by acknowledging and appreciating the things you love about yourself. This can include your personality traits, skills and talents, knowledge, style, choices, and your physical self. What do you admire about yourself? Is it your compassion? Your capacity for forgiveness and grace? Maybe it's the ways you've taken care of yourself and shown up for yourself, or your commitment to growth.

You can thank your body, health, and dedication to yourself today, for being alive. You can also appreciate your breath and the opportunity to live another day on this Earth. Speak to your unique qualities, skills, and what makes you *you*. The more specific you can be, the better you'll become at celebrating the things that make you wonderful.

Over the course of a year, I wrote twelve notes to myself—one every thirty days. I wrote to various versions of myself, including my future self, inner child, inspiration, past self, and current self. I also wrote to Mz. Anxiety (my anxious self), my emotions, and "a smol bit frantic" me. These notes served different purposes: Some kept me on track, others reminded me to keep going, some carried the voice of a cheerleader, and others spoke as a friend. I wrote to show myself the same love that I was showering on others, to connect more deeply with myself, and to practice self-expression and self-love. Through this practice, I learned to be kinder and more compassionate toward myself and to appreciate the different aspects of who I am. It also helped me appreciate who I once was and dream about who I will someday be.

CURRENT SELF

Writing a handwritten note to your current self offers benefits such as self-reflection, emotional well-being, motivation, goal setting, self-discovery, mindfulness, and gratitude. Through writing, you can connect with your thoughts and emotions, affirm your worth, set goals, explore your identity, stay present, cultivate appreciation, and navigate whatever you are going through. I wrote a handful of notes to my current self; here is one I wrote four months in:

> *Hey, you can do this. Find home within yourself. Keep meditating and reading. Step outside if you need to reset. Everything is working out for you. Practice gratitude. Keep writing your notes every day. Take care of yourself. Embrace change. Dance your way through. You can do hard things. You have done hard things before. Find the sweetness in every challenge. Keep moving forward. Keep improving. Have faith.*
>
> *I love you and I'm proud of who you are and who you're becoming,*
>
> *Kristen*

PAST SELF

Writing to your past self can help you reflect, heal, grow, and gain perspective on past experiences and lessons. I wrote this note while looking at one of my favorite photos of me as a child. I wanted to look at her and remember. I wanted to look at her and feel her presence, her essence, her voice, her kindness, her beingness. I cried when I wrote this one.

A note to my inner child:

Hi, little one.

I see you in there. Behind everything that has happened. Looking for love, for care, for tenderness. For acknowledgment when you are scared. For when life gets overwhelming or tough. I see the brightness in your eyes. The goodness in your soul. The innocence in your heart. I see your pure, perfect spirit. I promise to give you the attention and love you deserve. To take care of you. To keep you in mind when I am making decisions. To treat you the way you deserve to be treated. I am sorry for the times I got lost along the way. For the times I forgot. I know you are here and have always been here with me. Always a part of me. You are who I am. I promise to listen to you and give you what you need. You are with me and I am with you, little one.

I love you,
Kristen

FUTURE SELF

Writing to your future self can be a way to set goals, find motivation, stay accountable, and anticipate exciting future outcomes.

This is a note to my future self:

My wish for you is to truly believe you are enough. To live your life boldly with intention and passion. To make decisions with courage instead of fear. To listen to and trust your intuition. To respect yourself by setting and keeping boundaries. To find happiness from within. To keep practicing meditation and other ways to self-soothe. To contribute to the world. To keep growing, learning, improving, and expanding. May you shine bright and surround yourself with people you admire. May you practice gratitude every day. Remember to slow down and enjoy the present. Remember how far you've come. May you love every version of yourself along the way.

<3 KT

Another note to my future self:

My wish for you is to lean into every moment. To sit with your feelings. To be present in the present. To have fun. To enjoy the time in your life exactly how it is right now. Three decades have flown by. I remember wanting to be more grown-up or a different age. Always wanting something different, to be in another point in time, when I was "further along." This is it! The moment is now. The everlasting now. Let yourself live without dwelling in the past or fantasizing about the future. Surrender to reality and make decisions that align with your highest and best self. Listen to your intuition. Choose to be grateful every day. You have everything you need. I love you and I promise to keep loving you all the way through. Shine on, sis!

Your January 2022 self

Writing to . . . the Parts That Make You Whole

Writing to specific parts of yourself, like your inspiration, is a powerful practice that helps you connect with important aspects of your being. You can write to any "part" of yourself that might need attention or love. By embracing the parts that make up your whole self, you foster a deeper understanding and harmony within yourself.

A note to my inspiration:

To my inspiration,

Thank you. I enjoy my creativity! It is an honor to work together with you. To create notes. To foster ideas. To write.

I promise to make space for you in my life. To encourage imagination. To celebrate curiosity. To be open to what you have to offer. To welcome your ideas with excitement and gratitude. No matter how whacky or whimsical. To find delight in my work. To play along the way. To rejoice in your never-ending gifts. Life is juicier with you, my inspiration. Teamwork truly makes the dream work.

With love, your collaborator, admirer, and friend,
Kristen

You can write a note to yourself if you need a little pep talk. If you are facing challenges and need some extra love, give it to yourself. Treat yourself as you would treat your best friend. With TLC: tender loving care. Give yourself a hug—an actual hug *and* a hug in the form of a handwritten note. Everyone deserves a kind, handwritten note. Yes, everyone, especially you! Give yourself this gift.

So now you're jazzed about writing notes and can't wait to get started, right? Or maybe you're hesitating at this point.

I get it. Crafting a handwritten note can be exciting but also intimidating. If it makes you feel vulnerable, welcome to the club. It's completely normal, particularly when the expectations are high.

For example, a friend at my workshop shared that, for special occasions, her dad no longer desired material gifts. Instead, all he requested was a card with a handwritten note. As simple as this request was, it left her feeling overwhelmed. The pressure to do it right, to make it truly meaningful, weighed heavily on her.

Believe me, I have been there too.

But by embracing a systematic approach, I was able to address my concerns and establish a profound connection through my notes. The process I share in the coming pages makes looking at a blank card or page a little less intimidating and equips you with the necessary tools to craft a note that feels authentic and good.

Chapter Ten:

The Note-Writing Process

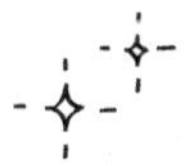

Do not fear, the how-to is here!

In this chapter, I present an easy-to-follow formula to intentionally connect with others through handwritten notes. The formula provides prompts and a menu of descriptive words to help you find your own language to authentically express how you feel. It invites you to tap into the specifics of your gratitude and appreciation and keeps your notes from sounding vague or generic.

I will walk you through the steps of the process, sharing the essential tips and tricks, insider knowledge, the quick and dirty details. Let me be your trusted guide as we delve into the depths of your emotions, unearthing words that will create a lasting impact. I will save you time by simplifying the process so you can stop worrying and get to creating. It's time to unleash your creativity and connect on a profound level through the power of the handwritten word.

A NOTE ON CREATIVITY

Before we dive in, a note on creativity—and having fun! Remember, a note doesn't have to be long or serious to be meaningful. Your notes can be short, silly, wild, wacky, whimsical, fun, dorky, quirky, concise, lengthy, or a combination of these. Your note can be a haiku, a poem, or a song. Your note can be an inside joke or written in a language only you and your recipient will understand.

Think of the following pages like a sandbox: a container that gives you enough structure to focus on the fun, playful, and expressive parts of this practice—and also grants you permission to kick to the curb anything that doesn't. It is always a choose-your-own-adventure.

You will know what is right to write. You will feel it, listen to your intuition, drop into your heart space, write with an open heart, and let your words flow through you. We will start with a freewrite followed by questions, prompts, words, phrases, and wishes to help you on your way. Use this how-to as a buffet to craft your own unique method and note.

A key takeaway from Elizabeth Gilbert's book *Big Magic* is that you already have the words within you to fill note after note. It takes courage to bring them forth, but by doing so, you can create magic and make meaningful change in the world. So keep an open heart, challenge yourself, and let your words flow freely.

A Step-by-Step Guide to a Note-Writing Practice

Here are the steps you can take on this journey:

STEP 1: Identify who (what, where) you want to write to.
STEP 2: Write about the note recipient.
STEP 3: Express gratitude for the recipient or acknowledge your reason for the note.
STEP 4: Describe how the person has affected your life.
STEP 5: Tell the recipient how they've made you feel.
STEP 6: Tell the recipient what you admire about them.
STEP 7: Share a personal connection.
STEP 8: End with a closing of well-wishes.

In this chapter, we will unpack each step with examples to jump-start your creativity.

Freewrite First

Before crafting the final message, I find it helpful to freewrite or journal as a way to get my feelings out. Depending on the circumstances, I either write by hand or type in the notes section on my phone or computer.

In my workshops, I encourage people to write for a duration of eight minutes (you can adjust this to fit your own style). At this stage, you don't need to worry about formatting, spelling, or grammar. Your journaling is solely for you. Its purpose is to bring forth what's within and release it.

Just as I do with my workshop participants, I invite you to engage with the following prompts to guide stream-of-consciousness writing about the person, place, or thing you intend to write to. This practice will help clarify your thoughts, identify exactly what you want to share, and determine precisely what you wish to convey to the recipient in the actual note.

STEP 1: Identify Who (What, Where) You Want to Write To

Remember, the recipient can be human, nonhuman, and even yourself. If you'd like to reflect on a place, thing, or animal, change the "who" to "what" or "where."

Dear ______________________

Use the questions below as a menu to identify the note recipient as you begin to brainstorm:

- Is there someone you are especially thankful for?
- Who made you smile?
- Who do you admire?
- Who has influenced your life?
- Who do you appreciate?
- Who showed you kindness?
- Who helped you?
- Who brightens your world?
- Who's made an imprint on your heart?
- Is there someone you want to thank?
- Who has enriched your life?
- Who could use your encouragement?
- Who have you lost touch with that you want to reconnect with?

- Who made you laugh?
- Who brings you joy?
- Who went out of their way for you?
- Who changed your life?
- Who believed in you?
- Who supported you?
- Who inspires you?
- Who do you want to share your words with?

People love to hear and see their own name, so it's important to ask for, listen to, and write down people's names. If you don't carry a pen and paper around, use your phone to keep track of names. This is especially crucial if you want to write a note to someone later on. Learn from my mistake—out of 365 notes, there's one where I forgot someone's name, and I regret it.

I was staying at the Loews Hotel in New Orleans when I became friends with the doorkeeper. We chatted every time I took my dog outside; he gave me restaurant recommendations, and I wanted to write him a note to say thank you. However, I didn't write down his name, and when I sent the letter, I had to address it to "the doorman." It didn't feel good, and I wish I had made the effort to remember his name.

When you write a note, make the extra effort to spell the recipient's name correctly both on the inside and outside of the card. This small detail can go a long way in making someone feel seen and valued. Give your note recipient the gift of showing them that their name is important enough to remember and spell correctly. It's a simple step that makes a big difference, and they will appreciate it.

HUMANS TO WRITE TO:

a family member you haven't spoken to recently, your partner, childhood friends, coworkers you'd like to get to know better, a coach or mentor, your boss, local and federal politicians, the barista at your favorite coffee shop, religious or spiritual leaders, first responders, activists in your community, poets, seniors in your community, a pen pal, park rangers, the host of a podcast you enjoy, janitors and custodians, flight attendants, volunteers, postal workers, a dance instructor, your babysitter or nanny, grocery clerks, vets and vet techs

NONHUMANS TO WRITE TO:

your pet or other animal, a city you love, your favorite place, somewhere you've lived, somewhere you want to travel to, the ocean, mountains, prairies, plants, a star, the wind, the seasons, a memory, a sound, a thought that crosses your mind, a feeling, a scent, God or the universe, a fictional character, an everyday object like your favorite mug or shirt, a sentimental object like a family heirloom or your baby blanket

STEP 2: Write About the Note Recipient

Reflect on your relationship with the note recipient and answer the following questions:

- What comes to mind when you think of this person?
- What does this person mean to you?
- How would you describe this person's energy?

- What do you want to express to them?
- What are all the things you appreciate about them?
- How do they make you feel?
- How have they impacted your life?
- What characteristics stand out to you?
- What makes this person unique and special?
- Can you capture their essence with specific words?
- What do you want to share with them?
- What do you wish for them?

Write whatever comes to mind. If you are thinking or feeling something, include it. Express your gratitude toward the person, appreciate them, and let them know what you admire about them. Share how they made you feel, how they uplifted you, and how they served as an inspiration to you. Write your true, genuine feelings. Recall special memories or moments you shared with them and reflect on the significance they hold for you, regardless of whether they were grand or seemingly small.

STEP 3: Express Gratitude for the Recipient, or Acknowledge Your Reason for the Note

Now we move into the heart of the note, where you share your thoughts, feelings, and wishes. Tell them the specific feeling you want to express. It might be gratitude, sympathy (for additional thoughts on sympathy notes, refer to the callout box in Chapter Nine), celebration, or any feeling you want to share.

Congratulations on ______________________________
Thank you for your help with ______________________
Thank you for __________________________________
I'm over the moon for you about ___________________
I appreciate your ________________________________

Questions to answer:

- Why are you writing to this person?
- What is the reason for the note?
- What are you grateful for?
- What are you celebrating?
- What do you appreciate?
- How did this person help you?

The list of things you might be thankful to them for really is endless. For example:

friendship, thoughtful gifts, making you feel less alone, picking you up from the airport, taking out the trash, cooking a meal, planning quality time together, having your back, brightening your day, believing in you, providing excellent service, being your chosen family, kindness, positive attitude, generosity, calming presence, openly sharing their journey, being a role model, killer dance moves, stellar book recommendations, quick wit and one-liners, advice, authenticity, ongoing support, shared memories, being fiercely themselves, dedication to community, using their platform for the greater good

STEP 4: Describe How the Person Has Affected Your Life

If you are called to write this person a note, I think it's safe to assume they have touched your life in some way. This step is to explain, in words, how they made an impact. How they enriched your life. How they left a footprint.

You have ______________________________
You helped me ______________________________
You changed the way I ______________________________
You showed me ______________________________
You taught me ______________________________
You brought ______________________ *into my life*
You gave me ______________________________
You inspired me to ______________________________
You encouraged me to ______________________________
You influenced ______________________________

To get to the heart of the matter, answer these questions:

- How has this person affected your life?
- How has this person enriched your life?
- How did this person make an impact on your life?
- How did this person touch your life?
- How did this person leave a footprint?
- What did this person bring into your life?
- What changed in your life because of this person?
- How did this person help you?
- What did you learn from this person?
- What did this person redefine for you?
- What did this person show you?
- How did this person assist your growth?

Dig deep to find the words to describe how they affected your life. And if you need some help, scan the phrases on the next page to see if anything fits.

changed the way I think, helped me embrace my weird, enriched my world, made me feel less alone, brought out the best in me, exceeded expectations, stood by me through a hard time, helped me face reality, showed me the joy of living, helped me find self-compassion, showed me anything is possible, inspired me to make a difference, made life easier, encouraged my creativity, gave me TLC, influenced my work, encouraged me to step up to challenges, gave me hope for the future, offered your understanding heart

STEP 5: Tell the Recipient How They've Made You Feel

Since this person affected your life, they probably had an emotional impact on you. This step gives you a chance to express those feelings. Let them loose! Tell the note recipient how they made you feel. No need to be shy.

You made me feel ______________________________
I feel ________________________ *when we are together*
I feel ___________________*after spending time with you*
Thank you for making me feel ___________________

To help you articulate your feelings, answer these questions:

- What feelings did you experience while spending time with this person?
- What feelings did you experience after spending time with this person?

If words are hard, below is another choose-your-own-adventure list. Choose the feeling that best describes how the note recipient made you feel. Bring those inside feels to the outside. If you see a feeling below that resonates, use it!

happy-hearted, safe, inspired, over the moon, unconditionally loved, seen, energized, full of wonder, at-home, curious, proud, understood, heard, wistful, hopeful, reassured, supported, peaceful, respected, jazzed, empowered, grounded, calm, cared for, rejuvenated, less alone, refreshed, confident, included, tickled, overjoyed, fired up, fabulous, validated, valued, appreciated, encouraged, desired, nurtured, cherished, optimistic, capable, playful, funny, motivated, fulfilled, lucky, worthy

STEP 6: Tell the Recipient What You Admire About Them

Express your gratitude for something specific and sincere about them or something they have done for you.

I appreciate your ______________________________
I appreciate how you ___________________________
I admire your _________________________________
I admire how you ______________________________
I love your ___________________________________
I love how you ________________________________
You inspire me to _____________________________
Your _____________________________ *inspires me*
You are a(n) _________________________________
You bring out ___________________________ *in me*
You add ____________________________ *to my life*

Find something to genuinely compliment. Use these questions to help you:

- What do you appreciate about this person?
- What do you admire about this person?
- What makes this person rad?
- What specifically makes you grateful for this person?
- What makes this person special?
- What makes this person unique?
- What talents do they have?
- What sticks out to you about this person?
- What shines through this person?
- What makes this person awesome?
- How does this person inspire you?
- What does this person bring out in you?
- What does this person add to your life?

Hey there, admiration station here! Let's rave about the note recipient by highlighting what makes them special. If any of the below words ring true, you know what to do.

grit, perseverance, strength, pizzazz, hilarity, vulnerability, openness, being a breath of fresh air, friendliness, kindness, faith, spirituality, creativity, outside-the-box thinking, ferocity, love of play, drive, poise, contagious passion, clear communication, empathy, candor, courage, resilience, guidance, reliability, resourcefulness, ingenuity, authenticity, eclectic taste, great hugs, heart-warming smile, acceptance, loveable nature, happy-go-lucky attitude, trustworthiness, tenderness, grace, professionalism, commitment to values, great parenting, mischief, radiant soul, leadership, loyalty, bravery, intelligence, work ethic, curiosity, positive outlook, infectious laughter, patience, integrity, captivating spirit, thoughtfulness, rock-solid sensibility, sense of style, spunk, silliness

STEP 7: Share a Personal Connection

Here lies your opportunity to share special memories and articulate the significance they hold for you. This reinforces the connection you have and shows that you were actively engaged in those moments. Don't forget to zoom in and include those specific details. Take the note recipient back to the moment with your words and sentiment.

I remember when ______________________________

I cherish our time together at _____________________

I will never forget ______________________________

I loved our time _______________________________

I hold our time __________________ *close to my heart*

Our memories _____________ *are some of my favorite(s)*

To help you think of shared experiences, conversations, or interests to write about, answer these questions:

- What is your favorite memory with this person?
- What shared experiences have you had with this person?
- What moments do you cherish with this person?
- What conversation with them still replays in your head?
- What memory will you never forget?

Ah, memories. Nostalgia is one of my favorite feels. These shared moments contribute to the unique bond you have with the recipient. Once you've reminisced on moments past, let's make this note official and send the recipient some well-wishes.

first meetings, coffee dates, vacations, sporting events, adventures, concerts, meaningful conversations, celebrations, milestones, perfect days out, venting sessions, births, deaths, inside jokes, DIY projects, movie nights, shared achievements, exploring new places, past embarrassments, phone calls, old photos, learning new skills, overcoming challenges, shared hobbies, family gatherings, holiday memories, support during hard times, special rituals, surprises, silly moments, weathering storms, late-night talks, witnessing natural wonders, deep conversations, overcoming a fear, volunteer work, raising a human, time with animals, finding hidden gems, transformative experiences, going dancing, sharing meals

STEP 8: End with a Closing of Well-Wishes

Finally, you'll sign off with a few words offering encouragement or support.

I wish you ______________________________
Wishing you ______________________________
May you ______________________________
May your ______________________________
May all your ______________________________
Sending you ______________________________

Think about this person in relation to current happenings or general support by answering these questions:

- What do you wish for this person?
- What do you hope they find?
- What do you hope they experience?
- What do you hope they receive?

According to Wikipedia, a well-wish is "an expression of positive regard and hope for good fortune." Share your positive desires, best wishes, and goodwill for the note recipient here.

Once again, the sky is the limit, so think big. Wish them the absolute best!

millions of dollars, the love of all puppies and kittens, wild amounts of fun, a life full of important fucks to give, the best year yet, continued success, the courage to dream big, health, wellness, fast healing, peace on their journey, for everything to go well, a big hug and kiss, rainbows and butterflies, all their wildest dreams to come true, a life full of joy and meaning, a year full of magic and wonder, the best life has to offer, a fun-filled fantastic decade ahead

On the cards I created, I included a lovingkindness mantra inspired by Sharon Salzberg in her book *Lovingkindness*. The lovingkindness mantra I use is:

May You Be Happy
May You Be Healthy
May You Live with Ease

I wish this for all my note recipients. I send this loving-kindness to them with my words, with my thoughts, and with my being. You can create your own lovingkindness mantra that feels true to you.

Last Words

Additional ideas for sign-off messages:

- With gratitude
- With love
- Love
- In friendship
- Thank you
- Best wishes
- Warm wishes
- Be well
- My best to you
- Yours truly
- All the best
- Peace
- Hugs
- Sending you a big hug
- Your friend
- xoxo
- Cheers
- Cheers to you
- Wishing you the best
- Take care
- With love and care
- Forever thankful
- Love you dearly
- All my love
- Happy holidays
- Peace and love
- Peace and blessings
- Hope to see you soon
- Cheering for you
- Respectfully
- Best

- Missing you
- In appreciation
- Cheering you on as you continue along your path
- With respect
- Miss you dearly
- Wishing you a joyful holiday/holiday season
- Wishing you continued success
- Wishing you continued success in all your endeavors
- Cheers to the best decade and adventures yet
- The best is yet to come
- All you need is already within you
- Sending you sunshine
- Until we meet again
- Onward and upward
- With admiration
- Wishing you a wonderful next chapter
- Your fan
- Sending you every good wish
- May all your flowers bloom
- Keep shining
- Sending awesome your way

Sit with It

Once you've completed your journaling/freewrite, let it sit for an entire day or at least a couple of minutes. Taking a break allows you to come back with fresh eyes and a new perspective when it's time to physically write the note. The break also helps you catch anything you might have missed and make any necessary edits from a different and clear state of mind.

Now you're ready to take what you freewrote and turn it into a note. How? Well, that's completely up to you! Your freewrite/journal/rough draft of a note is your guide. Pick and choose what feels right to include. This is when you can take a second pass through the steps if you'd like. After sitting on your rough draft, you can rewrite it or write something new altogether.

Unless I am in an extreme rush, I try to let my rough draft note sit for at least a day before revisiting it. When I return to it, I read it out loud to ensure that it conveys what I truly want to say. I make any necessary edits. Then, it's go time!

Gathering Supplies

This step is when you gather the necessary supplies for actually writing the note.

You'll need some kind of paper. You can use traditional paper or a card. Perhaps start with an old notebook, or get creative and make your own card. Choose something that reflects your personality and style while keeping the recipient in mind.

Next, choose your writing utensil. Choose a pen you enjoy and that is easy to write with. It should be comfortable to hold and bring you joy. Do you like gel pens? Do you like colored pens? Do you like glow-in-the-dark pens? I prefer gel pens, but ballpoint pens, fountain pens, and even pencils are available if you feel called. If you prefer to type your note first, gather your computer. Insider scoop: In my workshops, we write or type our words out and let them sit before we revisit them and write the actual note. And don't forget to have some Wite-Out on hand for do-overs.

If you'd like to write on a card, find one that feels right for your recipient. What does this card look like? Is it a thank-you note? Does it have a funny dog picture on it? Is it a sympathy card? Do you want to create your own card? If you prefer someone else to create it, the sky is the limit. You can find my greeting card sets, with eight full-color cards and envelopes, at www.creatively-noted.com. You can also find cards at your local card shop, Hallmark, online on Etsy, from your favorite creators, at the local drugstore, at the grocery store, from Paper Source, or even from Target. You can make your own cards. You can source an artist to design your own cards (I recommend Courtney Starbird at www.wildlittlecoyote.com) and send them to a local printer (I recommend Best Graphics, Inc. at info@bestgraphicsinc.com). Find something that feels right. If you can, buy or make extra. I have a green bag full of cards I carry around. I always have birthday cards on deck for last-minute occasions.

When you've found the perfect canvas, write your final draft there.

Above and Beyond: Take Your Note to the Next Level

You've done it! Your note has taken form! What's next? Looking to go pro in your note-writing? I'll help you level up in this section.

Proofread

It's important to proofread your handwritten note before sending it to ensure correctness. Check for any spelling, punctuation, or grammatical errors. Sending a note with errors is not representative of the care you are thoughtfully putting into it, so make sure your actions are aligned with your values and take the time to demonstrate that you are attentive to detail and take pride in your work. If you do make a mistake, don't worry—just have Wite-Out on hand.

After proofreading for correctness, read your note out loud to check for clarity. When you hear the words spoken, you'll be able to tell if they make sense and flow in the way you intend. This can help you identify any sentences or phrases that might be confusing or unclear. If necessary, revise your note to ensure that your message is conveyed clearly and effectively.

Document

Let's talk about documentation. Throughout my note-writing year, I kept a Word document with all of the notes I wrote as well as photos of the inside and outside of every card. I have a photo album on my phone of every note I've sent since I started this project. I highly recommend this for several reasons.

First, documenting your notes allows you to look back on what you've sent. It can be a source of joy to revisit the words and sentiments you've shared with others. You can review your notes as an active gratitude practice when you need some happiness in your life or when you are feeling low. Second, if a note gets lost in the mail and someone tells you they didn't receive it, you can easily send them a photo of the inside and outside of the note as proof of your efforts. It provides an extra layer of insurance, and while you can't control the mail, you can control your own documentation.

When my friend in Arizona hadn't received my carefully crafted love note, I was disheartened. Thankfully, I had photos of the card and texted her a copy. Documentation insurance to the rescue! Although it wasn't the same as receiving the physical card, she still got to experience my words and sentiment. I felt relieved. Despite the missing card, our connection deepened.

It might seem unnecessary, but documenting your notes is worthwhile; it benefits both you and the recipient. Taking photos of each card allows you to reflect on the positive effect you've had and serves as a means to reconnect if the recipient reaches out about the note. It's a simple step that can save you from potential hassle and help you track your progress. Believe me, you'll be glad you did.

Finishing Touches

Now comes the exciting part: adding those finishing touches to your handwritten note. Remember, bringing joy into the process is key, and now is your time to shine!

Consider incorporating some creative elements that will make the note extra special. One idea is to include a fun sticker that complements the message you want to convey. You could choose one that reflects a shared interest or inside joke, adding a touch of personalization. You could also consider including a memorable photo that captures a cherished moment between you and the recipient, evoking warm feelings and fond memories.

For an unexpected surprise, why not sprinkle a few colorful confetti pieces within the folds of the note? As the recipient unfolds it, they will be greeted with a joyful burst of confetti, setting a festive tone and making the experience even more delightful.

Here's a scent-sational suggestion: Invite the recipient to smell the scented ink of the pen you used. It's a small but spunky, fun detail that can add another layer of sensory pleasure to their reading experience. If you have a signature scent, you could even lightly spritz the note with your perfume or cologne, infusing it with your unique essence.

Do you have a knack for doodling or drawing? Now is the perfect time to showcase your talents. Add a fun design or personal touch that would be meaningful to the recipient. Whether it's a whimsical illustration, a heartfelt symbol, or a hand-drawn border, let your artistic flair illuminate the note to make it truly one-of-a-kind.

Consider what else you could include to make the note extra special for the recipient. Is there a small trinket, a pressed flower, or a meaningful quote that could accompany the message? This is your opportunity to fully express yourself and let your creativity flow. So go ahead and let your imagination run wild! Have fun with it, and enjoy the process of adding those finishing touches. Then send it off!

When it comes to postage, seek out a stamp that embodies your personality or that of the recipient. You can find stamps at your local post office or at USPS.com. You have a wide range of options to explore, from new and vibrant stamps to charming vintage ones. Choose a stamp that brings you joy or represents a shared interest. Personally, I enjoy using the "Garden Beauty" flower stamps. They never fail to delight me with their beauty, reminding me of my love for nature. They have everything from Walt Disney villain stamps to coral reef stamps to fruit and vegetable stamps. Go wild. Let your stamp choice reflect your personality and evoke a sense of happiness.

See, that wasn't so bad, was it? You followed the easy "how-to" formula and now you are intentionally connecting with others through handwritten notes. You have become an active participant in the handwritten-note revolution. You love-spreader, you! You battled with your pen and paper, you persevered through challenges, and you dedicated your time to fostering meaningful connections. You are changing the world, one note at a time. You rock!

How are you feeling? If you are experiencing any overwhelm, resistance, fear, or doubt, please know that you are not alone. The most common resistance I faced throughout the process was simply getting started. I hesitated to begin because, like you, my to-do list was never-ending, and I felt like I could be doing something more productive. The next chapter will provide you with guidance to overcome any obstacles you may encounter along your note-writing journey. Together, we can navigate through them.

Chapter Eleven:

Common Roadblocks and Detours

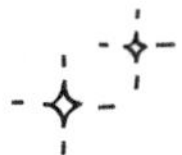

On your note-writing journey you *will* encounter real and imagined challenges. I encountered resistance, felt shame, and ran into ongoing potential roadblocks. Some days I didn't want to write a single word.

You will probably face those days too. Pretty much *everyone* faces these challenges when trying to establish a new habit or practice—I've heard as much from my workshop participants. Fortunately, there are ways to work through all of the different forms of resistance you're likely to meet.

In this chapter, I'd like to talk through some problems that might come up for you and teach you how to combat them. I will share the tools that helped me persevere through the note-writing process in hopes that they might help you, too, because I think the note-writing journey is worth pursuing and the benefits massively outweigh the struggles. You are capable of taking on this process. Everything you need is already within you.

Let's begin by asking: What are we afraid of?

I'm Afraid . . . I'm Not Creative Enough

When someone shares their roadblock to writing handwritten notes as "I'm not creative enough," I suggest shifting their mindset by removing the "not" and starting over with "I'm creative enough." It's important to recognize that everyone has the potential to be creative in their own way.

Here's the truth: You yourself are a creative miracle, with unique talents and perspective. With practice, you can strengthen your creative muscles and find your own creative voice. Try the funky lettering, throw in a rhyme, attempt a haiku, doodle a little ditty, or do anything else that speaks to you. Wear your heart on your sleeve, turn your insides out for the sake of creativity. Your creativity is with you, always, and it is eager to work with you.

I know it's easy to fall into the comparison trap, especially when we see the amazing creativity of others on social media. As I started my Creatively Noted Instagram and began following other snail mail and handwritten-note connoisseurs, I encountered bespoke calligraphy, vintage stamps, and custom stickers. I could easily have been discouraged if I'd compared their level of sophistication to mine. Instead, I let their creativity blow my mind. This is essential—don't be discouraged by the fancy flourishes of others. Instead, let their work inspire you to see that what is possible is endless.

If creativity is a concern, you should address it directly. Literally, write a note to your creativity. Share your intention to work together and ask for inspiration to flow. Make it a formal invitation. Ask your creativity to go easy on you because you are just learning. By partnering with your creativity, you can produce something truly unique and special. Your notes will be a representation and manifestation of you and your creativity. A creation collaboration. Be open to getting silly and following your heart and joy. And get ready to receive a taste of creative delight.

With the right mindset, anyone can learn to cultivate their creativity and use it to bring something new into the world, including handwritten notes. Don't let the fear of not being "creative enough" hold you back. I'm willing to bet you don't even know all the creativity you hold inside yourself, but you will see it once you begin to express it. Embrace your creativity and let it shine in your notes.

I'm Afraid . . . I Don't Have Time (to Write a Long Note)

The biggest challenge I've experienced and heard from others is time—actually sitting down and taking the time to physically write a note. We are busy. We want to write more notes, but we're faced with a long and growing to-do list to tackle, on top of working and trying to spend time with family and friends. The solution? Build a container for creation. Schedule it in to make it happen.

Your time is valuable, so it's crucial to prioritize human connection and treat note-writing as a meaningful use of your time. Despite your busy schedule, consider setting aside a designated time for note-writing. Even just five minutes a day can make a difference. Instead of engaging in unhealthy habits during your free time, use it as an opportunity to connect with others through heartfelt notes. Lose yourself down rabbit holes of appreciation and gratitude. By making a conscious effort to focus on life-giving outlets for your time, you can cultivate deeper relationships and enrich your own life as well.

And remember, your note doesn't have to be one long letter. It can be a haiku. It can be five words. What matters is not how much you write, but the connection you make with your words.

I'm Afraid . . . I'm Not in Touch with My Feelings

The majority of the note-writing process requires you to pull your feelings from the inside to the outside.

Easier said than done, amirite? Although this comes naturally to some, it often takes practice; fortunately, everyone can improve with practice. Let me assure you it is OK to feel whatever you are feeling; the full spectrum of feelings and emotions is allowed. Sometimes words can't fully describe your feelings and that's OK too. Language is limited; our emotions are not.

Some feelings are harder to pull than others. Once I got into feeling the essence of the person I was writing to, it was easier for me to expand upon my experience of them with words. I had to just go for it and strive to be as honest as possible.

Through your note-writing journey, you will have happy notes, sad notes, and everything in between. You will celebrate with others, and you might also sit with loss. This is normal and OK. Every day will be different; every note will be different. The only constant is change, and your feelings and emotions will fluctuate, making this process a little different every time you sit down to write. Challenge yourself to sit with your feelings and use your words to best express them with others, whatever that looks like specifically for you.

I'm Afraid . . . of How Others Will Respond

Sometimes it was scary to tell people how much I admired them. This sounds dumb, but it is true. Early on, I let go of how they would respond and reminded myself it was a practice for me. Benefiting others was awesome, but it was just a bonus. If someone thought a note was dumb, so be it. It was my special, unique creation and appreciation, and if it wasn't "cool" to them, then oh well. I would rather be kind than cool anyway. Also, I was simply too busy for the negative—I had work to do, notes to write, people to uplift!

You must intentionally let go of how people will respond. It is your job to express your feelings and self through note-writing. It is *not* your job to control their response. It doesn't matter how hard you try, you can't control anybody else's reactions anyway. So bring your responsibility back into the arena of what you can control. This means letting go of them responding to you at all—they may never acknowledge that you sent a note, regardless of how much time and thought you put into preparing it for them. You just have to realize that you did the work, and that is enough. You said what you needed to say. You crafted your words and feelings into a custom gift for them and gave it away. Take satisfaction in your effort and let the rest go. If they respond, great! If they don't, great!

I'm Afraid . . . I'll Get Bored

Boredom isn't bad. Sometimes you need to allow yourself to do nothing; this can be an essential part of the creative process. Although boredom does not seem like a creative feeling, it's a way of clearing our space for new ideas to spring up. Singer Wilson Pickett claimed resisting the quick fix and riding out his boredom was vital. As John D. Eastwood, coauthor of *Out of My Skull: The Psychology of Boredom*, told the BBC, "Boredom triggers mind-wandering, and then mind-wandering leads to creativity."[24] So put your phone and computer away in another room and set an alarm. Keep only your notebook, cards, and pen in front of you, and see what happens during that container of time.

---

24. Claudia Davis, "How Boredom Can Spark Creativity," *BBC Culture*, May 22, 2020, accessed April 30, 2025, https://www.bbc.com/culture/article/20200522-how-boredom-can-spark-creativity.

What I'm suggesting is that you create a container—some sort of structure—from which your inspiration can spring. It's a vital part of the process, and what comes next can actually be a lot of fun. For example, I've been working with my dad to install a Friday note-writing program at his office. He is going to cater lunch for whoever wants to participate in writing two handwritten notes. This is a fun way to write together, sharing ideas, relationship insights, and connection. He is building a container of time to create handwritten notes.

Similarly, I held a workshop for a residential real estate company and guided them through writing two handwritten notes using my process with prompts. After each note, we discussed insights and openly shared about the experience. As a bonus, it was a bonding opportunity. A way to practice vulnerability and connection. It was a way for colleagues to better get to know and understand each other and what was important to them.

It's possible to make this a fun, special, enjoyable event. The more the merrier. Creating a container for this practice benefits everyone who participates, the receivers, and more. The positive effects continue on and on.

I'm Afraid . . . I Just Can't Do It

Life starts when you meet your fears. Fear is information and opportunity.

When you experience resistance, I highly recommend reading *The War of Art* by Steven Pressfield. As he says, "The more important a call or action is to our soul's evolution, the more Resistance we will feel toward pursuing it." He also says, "If it meant nothing to us, there would be no Resistance." Note-writing—spreading love, uplifting spirits, and intentionally connecting—means something. It is important work.

You are going to feel resistance along the way, you are going to feel fear, and you are going to be OK. What you should fear most is leaving all of the notes that "could be" in your head. What you should fear is leaving a well-intended note unwritten. What you should fear is not ever taking the steps to tell people you love them, how you feel about them, what you admire about them. What you should fear is letting life pass you by without stopping to look around and share your admiration and appreciation. Life is short. If not now, when?

I'm Afraid . . . I'll Feel Ashamed

Shame. There was a time in my life, "the dark times," when I carried so much shame, I couldn't get out of my own way. I couldn't emerge from my self-pity enough to think about others. Heck, I was barely surviving myself. Moving through shame is tough work, but possible. If you are feeling shame, know that this note-writing exercise is a step in the direction of feeling better. Writing handwritten notes is an avenue for you to work through these unsettling feelings, to take action, and to find the good while tapping into your own light and that of others.

Give yourself the gift of reaching out and connecting to someone you love and trust. Give yourself the gift of writing to yourself and speaking to yourself the way you would speak to your best friend. For additional shame resources, please check out Brené Brown's work.

I'm Afraid . . . Nobody Even Cares

If you're feeling shy and letting your inner bully have a voice, believe me, I know what you're up against. I mentally questioned everything. Why bother writing to this person when they probably won't even read it? Who am I to write all of these notes? Who even cares about notes? This is a dumb idea. I'm dumb for doing this. Here is a note I wrote to myself on day thirty about resistance and giving up:

Kristen,

Thank you for showing up. Thirty days of handwritten notes of gratitude . . . an epic first month of learning and expression. Courage in uncharted waters. Thank you for listening to your calling and for taking action. Thank you for trusting your intuition and for not giving in to fear or resistance. Your work is meaningful and important. I'm proud of you and your commitment to your art. You are an artist! Keep creating. Keep expressing. Your words create a ripple effect you've only seen a glimpse of. Remember the smiles.

You are enough and I love you.

Kristen

Sometimes you have to pep talk your way through your fears and push forward anyway. To me, writing a note to myself every thirty days was a way to keep myself in check. It was a way to acknowledge myself, my feelings, what I was going through, and to have appreciation for myself through the journey. If you aren't jazzed about writing yourself a note, there are other ways of dealing with fear. You could journal to get out your thoughts or you could give your fear a name, make it some hot coffee, and settle it into a comfy seat while you finish your notes.

However you do it, here's your reminder to set the ego aside. Your ego isn't on the same team as our note-writing squad. Ego, you can't sit with us. We are busy changing the world one handwritten note at a time. And for when you're thinking outside of the box and your ego is trying to get in the way, you can turn to these words from *A Course in Miracles*, first published by the Foundation for Inner Peace in 1975: "Your ego and your spirit will never be co-creators, but your spirit and your Creator will always be. Be confident that your creations are as safe as you are."

I'm Afraid . . . I'm a Total Stranger

In note-writing, there's no such thing as "stranger danger." If you want to reach out to someone you don't know—an author, creator, musician, athlete, etc.—do it! This may take you a few extra steps, although there's often a way to reach them. Start by scanning their socials for any kind of address (mailing, email, etc.). There should be some form of contact information. If you can't find an address on any of their social media, take a picture of the front and back of the card and send it through whatever avenue they offer or you can find (email, website, Instagram, LinkedIn).

You don't need anyone's permission. You can give yourself permission to write a note to that person you really admire or look up to. You can give yourself permission to brighten someone's day. You can give yourself permission to be a game changer, to heal others and to heal yourself through increased deeper connection. You can give yourself permission to brighten the world around you, one note at a time.

I'm Afraid . . . of Actually Sending It

OK, so you've written your note, but you are filled with nerves. Sometimes I get nervous to send notes too. I get the jitters worrying about how the receiver will respond. If you truly do not want to send the note, then don't. If it was helpful for you to get your feelings out on paper and you want to leave it at that, then great. This is an opportunity to be completely honest with yourself. Do you truly feel called to send your note? If yes, don't let your nerves stand in the way. Let your intuition be your guide. Trust that you're being led in the right direction. To send or not to send? Remember, we are letting go of expectations here. The answer is in your heart and in your hands.

I'm Afraid . . . I Waited Too Long

It is never too late to write a note. Too many days have *not* gone by. You did not miss the window of opportunity. In fact, the more time that has passed, the more meaning the note could communicate—a note sent after some time has passed is proof that the recipient has made a lasting impact on your life, that the memory you made was meaningful and worth remembering.

I wrote a note to my friend's new baby. The baby had already grown a few months before I got around to sending the note. Did it stop me from sending it? No. Did I change some wording, since I had already, in fact, met that little angel? Yes. Did the note still have meaning, create a connection, and make them smile? Yes.

Many of my notes have been "late" or after the fact. Don't let the little voice tell you it's too late because it simply is not. For example, I wrote a note to a delightful server at Uchiko in Austin because she had the best energy—she was kind, funny, helpful, and spunky. My friend and I had a blast dining with her. Instead of sending off a note by mail right away, though, I waited until we went back so I could deliver it in person. She wasn't serving that day, but I sent my note to her in the back. As it turned out, the timing was perfect. She came out, almost in tears, to say thank you. "I was having a stinky, horrible day," she said.

The note was delivered exactly when it was meant to be, I'm sure of it. The sneaky thing you don't realize is that the universe is secretly working with you and your inspired action to deliver your notes full of love. It's never too late; in fact, it's just the right time.

I'm Afraid . . . My Handwriting Sucks

"But my handwriting is bad!" I hear it all the time. And maybe you don't love your handwriting. That is OK. Everyone starts somewhere. Even if handwriting doesn't come naturally or easily at first, you can always build upon and strengthen your skills. We love improving! Great news: Practicing writing is the best way to get better at writing.

It's worth putting in the time to practice, because your handwriting is a gift that's uniquely yours. It's an expression of you. Use this gift and it will get even better. When you practice writing handwritten notes, your handwriting is guaranteed to improve and—who knows?—you may even grow to love and appreciate it. You will never know until you try. Instead of resisting and fighting it, you can choose to work with it as a teammate. Repeat this with me: "I love my handwriting, for it allows me to express my words and my love."

And remember, you can write as many rough drafts as you need. Don't give up! You will be so proud once you see the note you crafted! Fun tip: You can always send a handwritten note and a typed note with it if you are worried they won't be able to read it.

I'm Afraid . . . I Messed Up

Sometimes your handwriting will be too big for the page, and sometimes it will be too small. Sometimes it will start big and end small or the opposite. You will misspell words and mess up the spacing. You will accidentally write upside down. You will spill your coffee or leave a food mark. Shit happens. It's likely you will also encounter a cramped hand from writing. A wasted envelope. It will take longer than you think.

I call these writing pains. Note-writing is a lost art for a reason. You are one of the few willing to go the extra mile to create one-of-a-kind, meaningful masterpieces. We can do hard things; we can persevere for the sake of creation and connection. If you need to take a rest and revisit your note, do so. Otherwise, give yourself a little hug, take a few deep breaths, and continue on your note-writing way.

No Excuses

Creating a lasting habit is about commitment, not perfection. Sometimes the roller coaster of life will throw us off course, but we can always get back on track. Here are some excuses I've heard (and made!) that are completely within our power to overcome.

But . . . I'm Not at Home

But I'm traveling! This is a challenging, but not impossible, time to write notes. When I travel, I take advantage of the notes section on my phone. After a nice meal, epic adventure, or tour, I make sure to type in the name of whoever I want to write a note to. I also type the "rough draft" of their note in this section. This is a quick and easy way to capture your immediate feelings about this person and/or experience. You can save these "rough drafts" to physically write when you are back with your notes or no longer on the go.

But . . . I Missed a Day

So you set out to write a note every day and you missed a day. Breathe. Your life will continue, and everything is going to be OK. I understand the stress you are feeling because I fell asleep early one night, missing my note on day 333. As I mentioned earlier, I wrote myself a note every thirty days, and I took this as an opportunity to write to myself because I needed it.

My 333rd note, to “a smol bit frantic” me:

> *I am writing this the morning after. I am giving myself grace instead of having a meltdown. That is my choice response. It is OK. You are OK. It is enough. You are enough. Carry on with your mission. Give yourself a hug. Show yourself the same love and understanding you would show any of your friends or family. Let. It. Go. This is number 333, “an indication that the road ahead is open for you to continue on your journey.” About one month left. Let’s finish strong . . . with sincerity and heart. I am proud of your dedication and commitment.*
>
> *Keep writing. I love you.*

I don’t think it was a coincidence this was the only note I missed. The number three is associated with growth. The appearance of the angel number 333 indicates a positive energy toward your quest. Seeing my note number was 333 meant it was my time to expand. This was my not-so-subtle hint from the universe.

If you miss a day, take it and use it to make a mindset shift! This is not a roadblock or a sign of failure. It is an opportunity to grow and encouragement to shake it off and continue on your note-writing journey. You are doing something amazing. Carry on.

But . . . I Need Different Supplies

"But the supplies are not readily available in my everyday life," you say. You don't have the money to buy the supplies. Inflation, amirite?

Don't be distracted from your mission. You don't need fancy cards or fancy pens or fancy stamps to make meaning. You don't need ten-dollar cards. You can make your own with something as simple as computer paper. You could write on a loose-leaf piece of paper and fold it up in a fun way. Do you have an old notebook lying around the house? Put its pages to good use! Write on the back of a bill . . . might as well turn it into some joyful material! Bonus extra credit points for reducing, reusing, and recycling!

Your intention, attention, and words are what matter. The rest of it is just fluff. Don't let the extras stop you from moving forward and creating meaning. Your impact comes from your words, not how cute your pens are, although I love a scented pen.

But . . . I'm Not Sure Who to Write To

But, you might be thinking, *I don't have anyone or anything to write to!* I can relate. I too was worried I would run out of people to write to. How many people did I actually know? Did I realistically have words to share with 365 people?

If you are stuck in this challenge, have no fear. Start free-writing, journaling, and stream-of-consciousness writing to the prompt "I am thankful for ____________." Let your pen go wild on the paper. Start writing everything you are thankful for. You will find your way there. Nothing is too silly or small to be thankful for. You can be thankful for having a place to sleep and socks to keep your feet warm, for your morning coffee, the flowers for blooming, and the sun for shining down on you; you can be thankful to the farmer for growing your food, the mail carrier for delivering your notes, the person who helped you find something at the grocery store, your parents for giving you life, your neighbor for keeping watch over your house, your coworker for greeting you with a smile. As we've seen, it does not have to be a person. You can write to a place, an animal, or an inanimate object. Freewrite or journal until you discover what or who you want to write to.

To help my future decision-making self, I created a list of people "to write to" in the notes section in my phone, so if I woke up clueless one day, I could check my list. This list grew and continues to grow. Through this note-writing journey, I've realized there are *plenty* of people to put on this list. Originally, I was just imagining family and friends, but it's expanded to include people I have daily conversations with, like gym attendants and waiters. Also on the list are people who have influenced my life with their work, even if I've never met them before—like the founder of Orangetheory Fitness or my favorite author.

I've never run out of people to write to. When I reached the end of my year of note-writing, there were still so many more I wanted to write to! I got to the end of this challenge, and I am still writing handwritten notes. The gratitude never ends.

But . . . I Don't Have Anything Special to Say

I'm willing to bet you *do* have something special to say, no matter how it feels. It's true, as Elizabeth Gilbert tells us to remember in *Big Magic*, that sure, most things have been said or written before. But not by you. Not in your way. Not in your words. You are special. Maybe you simply haven't noticed what's special in your world. Or, as Sophia Joan Short puts it,

"Maybe the amount of extraordinary things that happen in your life . . . depends on what you notice."[25]

Writing notes helps us notice the wonder, the love, and the miracles surrounding us at all times. If only we had the eyes to see. If only we took the time to pay attention. To devote ourselves to appreciation. To devote ourselves to noticing the good. Looking back on the notes I've written, I get overwhelmed by the people that have appeared in my life. The joy they've brought me. The little things that are actually big things. A smile, a shared meal, a belly laugh, a friendship. My challenge for you is to notice these things because, as Jessica Hagy says, "You have treasured people, places, and things. They are precious and powerful. Fight for them. Don't just let them lounge in the back of your mind. A love ignored will wither and die."[26]

But . . . I'm Still Afraid . . . What Impact Could I Possibly Have?

This may be *the fear* behind all of our other fears about putting our words out into the world this way—that it won't matter. Believe me, after writing 365 notes, and receiving so many responses, I know it makes a difference. Imagine how it feels to get a response like this:

> *OMG I received your card today. Thank you so much for making a gloomy day brighter! I love and miss you!*

---

25. Sophia Joan Short, "Noticing with Sophia Joan Short," *HOKA*, October 4, 2023, https://www.hoka.com/en/us/blog-post/?id=noticing-with-sophia-joan-short.
26. Jessica Hagy, How to Be Interesting (Workman Publishing Company, 2013), 79.

That was a reply from my dance teacher when I was growing up. She received her note on the same day she wrecked her car, Pearl.

I can't make this timing up. Divine timing is on your side. Be open to the messages you are receiving. Are you called to write someone a note that is a blast from the past? Someone who inspired you? Gave you advice that you live by? Listen to the little voice guiding you, and trust that you are being guided.

Remember, every day is different, and every note will be different. Your note can be whatever feels true to you. Don't compare your notes to my notes or anyone else's notes. This means length, format, content, etc. Through practice, you will develop your own style of note-writing, *and* it will continue to develop and change through every note you write. The important thing is that you write truly and with an open heart. That you tap into your intuition, your creativity, your inspiration. That you work together with them to create meaningful notes with the truest words you can write in order to see the person you are writing to. That you are using words to meet the recipient where they are.

Also remember you are meeting each other anew through your note. You are finding shared, common humanity and beingness. You are using your words intentionally to create meaningful connection. To deepen your relationship and understanding of one another. To acknowledge that we are all on this journey together. Your words are magic. Your words can create feeling. Your words can inspire, delight, and comfort. Your words can move mountains. Believe in the power of your words. Write with power. Harness the truth and write it down. You have the power to change the world with your words. With your notes.

Conclusion

"It was clear that their most precious memories were forged from a collection of ordinary moments, and their hope for others is that they would stop long enough to be grateful for those moments and the joy they bring."

—Brené Brown, *The Gifts of Imperfection*

After looking back at my 365 notes, I am truly overcome with love. Rereading my notes brings me to tears. I have been given the most amazing people to share life with. I have been given a wonderful life. To think I have spent days depressed in my room, lost in self-pity and shame, is wild. I realize now, I was just lost. I had forgotten how to use my eyes to look around, to look inside, to see the gifts, to see the love. Notes helped me reconnect. They were my lifeline back to myself, my life, and everything that made it worth living: the people, the places, the experiences, the goodness. Sometimes I still get lost, but notes help me find my way back to myself, to the beauty of life, to the love surrounding me at all times, to the gifts big and small . . . if only I would slow down and take a moment to see. I never imagined what the 365-day note-writing journey actually had in store for me; in the end, the power of this practice blew my mind. The notes helped me appreciate, they helped me heal, they helped me connect more deeply with myself, they helped me forge deeper connections with my fellow humans and the world around me. Because of my notes, I am forever changed. My notes were the gift to myself I didn't know I needed. And as a bonus, they were a gift to others too!

And now, I have a chance to write one more note—to you!

Dear reader,

Challenge yourself to find a reason to be grateful. Challenge yourself to find a reason to write a note. At the beginning of my 365 notes, I was worried I would run out of people to write notes to, ha! Some of my best notes are the ordinary notes: thanking my parents for picking me up from the airport, thanking my partner for taking care of our house and taking on projects, thanking my coworkers for being good associates and friends, thanking waiters for their service. Although these are simple acts, they are worth appreciating. They are important. They matter. They are worthy of praise. They are worthy of a note!

As we've seen, human connection is nature's medicine. Attention is love. We can give this gift to others and to ourselves. With handwritten notes, we can heal, and we can love. And in life, aren't those really the point? To make life a little easier for everyone, to find our shared humanity, and to love? The big secret of note-writing has been revealed. It was lost, and now it's been found. The call to connect is now. The information and skills are now in your hands. Will you answer the call to write a note? Will you step up to the challenge? Will you be a note-writing warrior, spreading love and notes across the world? Sprinkling your magic and brightening the world one note at a time? Will you see for yourself if, truly, a note would help?

I challenge you to meet your note-writing self head-on. To welcome your note-writing self with open arms, to be open to the person note-writing will help you become. I challenge you to step into the next level of you. The one who takes the time to write a note, who makes time for the magic, who creates the magic.

I challenge you to set aside time for this intentional practice, to commit to it fully and to be open to receiving the massive benefits. Writing a note will help you in ways you can only imagine. Buckle up for the ride.

I also challenge you to push your language to the max. To use your words to the best of your ability to connect with others. To see them. To meet them where they are and find a common thread. Weave those threads together to create something that takes up its own existence—a blanket that can keep you warm, comfort you, and support your new-found interconnectedness.

Words are power. Written words can nurture a deep bond, which can lead to a sense of oneness and shared beingness. Use your words as tools to reflect your inner world, your inner feelings. Respect words and use them as building blocks to create stronger relationships. Write words to build connection. To create something greater than the words themselves. To string them together to create something so powerful, it cannot be described, for it fosters a feeling—a connection so deep, it cannot be fully explained with words, only felt. Something larger than yourself.

I challenge you to use today to be your day of greatest appreciation. I challenge you to use your words today to make this your day of greatest presence. I challenge you to use your words to make this your day of greatest awareness.

And I challenge you to do the same thing tomorrow too. And the day after that, by creating a note-writing practice. A practice of gratitude, creativity, thoughtfulness, and appreciation. Set aside the time. Not to hold yourself to an impossible standard, but to demonstrate your commitment to an ongoing practice that makes sense to you. One note per week is not too much to ask. One note per day can be done if you're up for it. A note per day for thirty days is a valiant effort.

I challenge you to step outside your comfort zone. I challenge you to step inside your vulnerability. I challenge you to write with an open heart. I challenge you to set aside time for your creations and inspirations to come to life. I challenge you to harness your insides and bring them to the outside with a pen and paper.

Decide how exactly you are going to challenge yourself with your note-writing practice, and let's go. With note-writing, your challenges will lead to transformation: of yourself, your relationships, and how you show up in the world around you. The cost—the time, the energy—is worth it.

When there are a million other things you could be doing, take the time to write a note. It is a gift you give others and a gift you also give yourself. Your commitment is what makes this gift so valuable. Despite everything vying to take away your attention, you are recognizing the gifts around you.

Do not underestimate how much you and your handwritten notes are needed. Write the note, be the blessing, start the ripple effect of love. I challenge you to write a note: a personal note, a professional note, a note to someone who made an impact on your life, a whimsical note, a note to a family member, a note to a neighbor, a note to an unexpected person, a note to a young person, a note to an old person, a note to an animal, a note to a place, a note to yourself, a note to a business owner, a note to your hero, a note to someone who inspired you, a note to someone who believed in you. I challenge you to write that note, the one on your mind right now. I challenge you to write the note you have been putting off. I challenge you to take the time to write that note. Write it, and report back. I want to know how the experience was. How was the process? How did writing the note make you feel? Please share your note-writing experience with me at kristen@creatively-noted.com.

Kristen Reiter
PO Box 40723
Austin, TX 78704

And in the End

In a world full of war, violence, and fear, I choose love. The handwritten-note revolution has begun. We can be the light. What we do matters. We can remind others of our shared humanity. Of our goodness. Of our oneness. That we are all neighbors in this world and although different, we share a common humanity. To love and to be loved. Underneath it all, isn't that what we are all looking for?

Our weapons are our notes. We are going into battle with pen and paper. Sending out love bombs. Nuking the unsuspecting hearts of others with kindness, appreciation, value, and delight. Being vulnerable, and in turn prying those armored souls wide open to love. We use our weapons of words to show the world there is another way. Note warriors fight for peace and love for all living beings. Note warriors fight for the Earth, all its inhabitants, and beyond. Love is the most powerful force in the universe. Align yourself with love.

I've written my own handwritten notes and will continue to. I've upped the ante now to encourage others to write their own meaningful handwritten notes. I envision the world becoming more interconnected and loving. Humans feeling more seen and acknowledged.

I see humans receiving handwritten notes in the mail, maybe even more than bills! Overwhelmed with belonging to their people, their community. Humans knowing they are a part of something greater, that their relationships are meaningful, that they are important, that they are loved.

You are ready, full of knowledge and power, to craft your own handwritten notes. The notes are already within you. You have all you need. It's time to pull those words from the inside out. Remember, if you ever feel lost or confused, you can refer to the "how-to" process as a guide. But feel welcome to forge your own path, whatever gets you to your truth, your authentic expression. Trust your intuition and follow your inner guidance. This is the way.

Let's fill the world with love and handwritten notes, together. As Pollyanna as it sounds, I truly feel like I was called to spread more love and joy around the world. Note-writing is an easy and simple way to do that. For me, for you, for everyone. And if we can bring a little more joy and love to the modern digital world, well, how about that? Note warriors, this is your calling. You are needed. Gather your supplies: your glitter pens, your stickers, your big hearts, your cards. Prepare your doodles. It's time. It's our time. The handwritten-note revolution is here. It's your time to shine.

Sources

Allen, Summer, PhD. "The Science of Gratitude." *Greater Good Science Center* (2018): 28–40. https://ggsc.berkeley.edu/images/uploads/GGSC-JTF_White_Paper-Gratitude-FINAL.pdf.

Brown, Brené. *The Gifts of Imperfection: Anniversary Edition*. Random House, 2020.

Burkeman, Oliver. *Four Thousand Weeks: Time Management for Mortals*. Picador Paper, 2023.

Daily Mail Online. "You Haven't Got Mail." October 3, 2011. www.dailymail.co.uk/news/article-2044652/Average-US-households-receive-personal-letter-just-7-weeks.html.

Davis, Claudia. "How Boredom Can Spark Creativity." *BBC*. May 22, 2020. Accessed April 30, 2025. https://www.bbc.com/culture/article/20200522-how-boredom-can-spark-creativity.

De Mello, Anthony. *Awareness: Conversations with the Masters*. Crown Publishing, 1992.

Emmons, Robert. "Why Gratitude Is Good." *Greater Good Magazine*. November 16, 2010.

Fredrickson, Barbara. "The Role of Positive Emotions in Positive Psychology." *American Psychologist* 56(3), 218–26. doi: 10.1037//0003–066x.56.3.218.

Gikandi, David Cameron. *A Happy Pocket Full of Money*. Xlibris, 2008.

Gilbert, Elizabeth. *Big Magic*. Riverhead Books, 2015.

Gilbert, Jack. "A Brief for the Defense." *Collected Poems*. Alfred A. Knopf, 2012.

Hagy, Jessica. *How to Be Interesting*. Workman Publishing Company, 2013.

Haig, Matt. *The Comfort Book*. Penguin Life, 2021.

Hanson, Rick. *Buddha's Brain: The Practical Neuroscience of Happiness, Love, and Wisdom*. New Harbinger Publications, 2009.

Hartman, Christie. "Loneliness Statistics: By Country, Demographics & More." *The Roots of Loneliness Project*. June 9, 2023. https://www.rootsofloneliness.com/loneliness-statistics.

Hepburn, Matthew. "Daily Gratitude Booster." Ten Percent Happier App, 2023. Podcast. https://www.poorstuart.com/podcast-episode/Ten-Percent-Happier/The-Massive-Power-of-Not-Taking-Sh*t-for-Granted-B/493510/.

Heschel, Rabbi Abraham Joshua. "Radical Amazement." *Awakin.org*. Accessed April 1, 2025. https://www.awakin.org/v2/read/view.php?tid=1080.

Hill, Napoleon. *Outwitting the Devil: Secrets to Freedom and Success*. Sound Wisdom, 2020.

Holiday, Ryan. *The Daily Stoic: 366 Meditations on Wisdom, Perseverance, and the Art of Living*. Portfolio, 2016.

Hyman, Mark. "Gratitude Heals." *DrHyman.com*. 2018. https://drhyman.com/blog/2018/12/04/gratitude-heals/.

John, Jaiya. *Daughter Drink This Water*. Soul Water Rising, 2018.

Jung, Carl. *Memories, Dreams, Reflections*. Vintage Books, 1989.

Jung, Carl. *Synchronicity: An Acausal Connecting Principle*. Princeton University Press, 2010.

Lambert, Nathaniel M., Margaret S. Clark, Jared Durtschi, Frank D. Fincham, and Steven M. Graham. "Benefits of Expressing Gratitude: Expressing Gratitude to a Partner

Changes One's View of the Relationship." *Psychological Science* 21, no. 4 (2010): 574–80.

Manson, Mark. "One Thing Has the Greatest Impact on Your Life." *Your Next Breakthrough*. December 26, 2022. https://markmanson.net/breakthrough/002-one-thing-has-the-greatest-impact-on-your-life.

Mill, John Stuart. *The Classic Autobiography of John Stuart Mill*. Liberal Arts Press, 1957.

Moran, Joan. "Pause, reflect and give thanks: the power of gratitude during the holidays." *UCLA: Newsroom*. October 29, 2013. https://newsroom.ucla.edu/stories/gratitude-249167.

Murthy, Vivek, MD. *Together: The Healing Power of Human Connection in a Sometimes Lonely World*. Harper Paperbacks, 2023.

Pressfield, Steven. *The War of Art*. Black Irish Entertainment LLC, 2002.

Rogers, Fred. *The World According to Mister Rogers: Important Things to Remember*. Hachette Books, 2019.

Rubin, Gretchen. *The Happiness Project*. Harper Paperbacks, 2018.

Salzberg, Sharon. *Lovingkindness*. Shambhala, 2020.

Salzberg, Sharon. *Real Love*. Flatiron Books, 2017.

Schucman, Helen, and Bill Thetford. *A Course in Miracles*. The Foundation for Inner Peace, 1975.

Seppala, Emma, PhD. "Connectedness & Health: The Science of Social Connection." *The Center for Compassion and Altruism Research and Education*. May 8, 2014.

Short, Sophia Joan. "Noticing with Sophia Joan Short." *HOKA*. October 4, 2023. https://www.hoka.com/en/us/blog-post/?id=noticing-with-sophia-joan-short.

Siegel-Acevedo, Deborah. "Writing Can Help Us Heal from Trauma." *Harvard Business Review*. July 1, 2021. https://hbr.org/2021/07/writing-can-help-us-heal-from-trauma.

Stahl, Ashley. "Here's How Creativity Actually Improves Your Health." *Forbes*. July 25, 2018. https://www.forbes.com/sites/ashleystahl/2018/07/25/heres-how-creativity-actually-improves-your-health/.

Waldinger, Robert, and Marc Schulz. "The Real Secret of Lifelong Fulfillment." *The Wall Street Journal*. February 3, 2023. https://www.wsj.com/story/the-real-secret-of-lifelong-fulfillment-6c1d026a.

Ward, William Arthur. *For This One Hour*. Droke House, 1969.

Wright, Victoria (@veekster). "If you are moved by someone, by someone's work, by their friendship, anything—TELL THEM." Twitter (now X). May 19, 2021. https://twitter.com/veekster/status/1395080305761918976?lang=en.

Zuckerman, Arthur. "40 Direct Mail Statistics: 2020/2021 Behavior, Trends & Data Analysis." *CompareCamp.com*. May 21, 2020. https://comparecamp.com/direct-mail-statistics/.

Acknowledgments

I want to express my heartfelt gratitude to the incredible people who have been instrumental in making this book a reality. Their support, insights, and encouragement have been the driving force behind this journey.

To my friends from the former Scribe: Emily, Chas, Gail, and Hussein, your guidance was a beacon through the challenging process of writing a book, and I can't thank you enough.

My sincere appreciation goes out to my workshop table, Jeff, Tim, Shelley, and Shubber, who believed in my book when it was just a seed of an idea.

Rose, your publishing expertise, proposal help, and thoughtful recommendations on how to move forward were truly invaluable.

Sheila, the ultimate professional who brought my book to life, I am eternally grateful. Your ability to understand my book and make it so much better is beyond words. Your beautiful work is evident on every page.

To my diligent copy editor, Marie, your expertise elevated this book to the next level. Your guidance and emotional support were equally as valuable through the challenging final stages of editing and publishing.

Ami, I appreciate you and your excellent copywriting skills, which made my book assets interesting.

To Brooke, Megan, Tabitha, Leah, Krissa, and the She Writes Press team, your guidance and indispensable contributions helped bring this book into the world. Thank you. To Tess, you went far beyond a typical proofread—thank you for your thoughtful and truly exceptional work. I'm forever grateful.

To some of my dearest friends and beta readers, thank you for your willingness to read my early drafts and for providing valuable feedback, which played a huge role in shaping this book. Caitlin and Annie, I hold our almost-twenty-year friendship close to my heart. Thank you for standing by me through every phase of my journey. Lynette, we expand together. Thank you for your unwavering belief in me. You are truly a wellspring of inspiration. Kasey, your friendship and support throughout this journey have kept me afloat. Thank you for providing laughs (and rhymes) every step of the way.

Cassandra, thank you for generously sharing your talents to bring my book, business, and dreams into reality. Your creativity inspires me, and your friendship fuels me.

Kristie, your ability to bring my visions to life through design is nothing short of remarkable. Your artistic ability, understanding, and enthusiasm are indispensable.

To my family: Mom and Dad, your love and support are my anchor. I deeply treasure your presence and help through the highs and lows, more than words can express. You have sacrificed and given over and over again for me. I am forever grateful. To my brother, Andrew, your sense of humor and wit add laughter to my life, and my sister, Elise, your companionship and love sustain me. Thank you.

Austin, you've been my pillar, my "secure base" of support, from the beginning. When I first conceived the idea to write 365 notes, your challenge to see it through was the catalyst for this book. This book wouldn't exist without you. I love you, thank you.

Mr. (Richard) and Mrs. (Polly), thank you for welcoming us into your home with open arms during our time of limbo and for your endless love and support. Abby, thank you for your friendship and genuine enthusiasm about my note-writing and book.

Bek, your unbelievable generosity led me to write you a note, and your feedback gave me the idea to start writing more notes and in turn, this book.

My coworker, Adam, thank you for your ongoing help and kindness lightening my load at our real estate job while I followed my dreams.

Cooper, you inspired me, showed me that publishing a book was possible, and encouraged me to move forward with my own.

I extend my heartfelt thanks to those whose comments are featured in this book and to all the authors whose quotes have enriched its pages. I am your devoted fan.

To everyone I've ever written a note to and who's written a note to me. Thank you for being a part of my journey. You made a meaningful impact and have helped me grow into the person I am today.

I'm deeply appreciative of all those who have touched my book in various ways, helping it evolve and grow. Your contributions, regardless of size, have left a lasting mark.

Lastly, to everyone who believed in me and offered words of encouragement along the way, you were my guiding lights. Without your support, this book would not have been possible. From the bottom of my heart, thank you.

About the Author

Writer and workshop leader Kristen Tremonti Reiter is the founder of Creatively Noted, dedicated to furthering authentic connection and self-development through handwritten note-writing. Her popular in-person and virtual note-writing workshops guide people to explore their creativity and engage with each other in unique, meaningful ways. Her passion for embracing the joy of creative expression while spreading love to others is contagious. An alumna of Kansas State University, Kristen lives with her husband, three-time Super Bowl Champion Austin Reiter, and their American Staffordshire Terrier mix, Sosa. She calls both Austin, Texas, and Fairway, Kansas, home.

Find out more at www.creatively-noted.com.

Looking for your next great read?

We can help!

Visit www.shewritespress.com/next-read
or scan the QR code below for a list
of our recommended titles.

She Writes Press is an award-winning
independent publishing company founded to
serve women writers everywhere.